U0483703

符号中国 SIGNS OF CHINA

秦始皇陵

THE MAUSOLEUM OF QIN SHIHUANG

"符号中国"编写组 ◎ 编著

中央民族大学出版社
China Minzu University Press

图书在版编目(CIP)数据

秦始皇陵：汉文、英文 /"符号中国"编写组编著. —北京：中央民族大学出版社，2024.9
（符号中国）
ISBN 978-7-5660-2314-8

Ⅰ.①秦⋯　Ⅱ.①符⋯　Ⅲ.①秦始皇陵—介绍—汉、英　Ⅳ.①K878.8

中国国家版本馆CIP数据核字（2024）第017484号

符号中国：秦始皇陵 THE MAUSOLEUM OF QIN SHIHUANG

编　　著	"符号中国"编写组
策划编辑	沙　平
责任编辑	黄修义
英文编辑	邱　械
美术编辑	曹　娜　郑亚超　洪　涛
出版发行	中央民族大学出版社
	北京市海淀区中关村南大街27号　邮编：100081
	电话：（010）68472815（发行部）　传真：（010）68933757（发行部）
	（010）68932218（总编室）　　　　（010）68932447（办公室）
经 销 者	全国各地新华书店
印 刷 厂	北京兴星伟业印刷有限公司
开　　本	787 mm×1092 mm　1/16　印张：9
字　　数	110千字
版　　次	2024年9月第1版　2024年9月第1次印刷
书　　号	ISBN 978-7-5660-2314-8
定　　价	58.00元

版权所有　侵权必究

"符号中国"丛书编委会

唐兰东　巴哈提　杨国华　孟靖朝　赵秀琴

本册编写者

戚嘉富

1978年4月，美国《国家地理》杂志以庞大的篇幅，图文并茂地登载了著名撰稿人奥黛丽·托品的文章《令人难以置信的奇迹》："历史上的这位胜利者就是秦始皇，他是中国第一位皇帝，也是万里长城的建造者。公元前210年，他被葬于一座称为骊山的、相当于15层楼高的大丘之

In April 1978, Audrey Topin, renowned staff writer in *National Geographic* took several pages and plentiful beautiful pictures to introduce the Mausoleum of Qin Shihuang to readers throughout the world, as quoted in her famous article *The Incredible Miracle*: "Qin Shihuang, the conqueror, was the first emperor in Chinese history, as well as the conductor in the construction of the Great Wall. In 210 B.C., he was buried under Lishan Mountain which was as high as a 15-floor building..."

The Mausoleum of Qin Shihuang is the first imperial mausoleum in China, and also the one with the largest architectural scale, the most distinct structure and the most diverse significance.

There lies the mysterious underground palace which still remains unexcavated and thousands of unearthed terracotta warriors. The life-size clay figurines, with various

1

下……"

秦始皇陵是中国历史上第一个皇帝陵园，也是世界上规模最大、结构最奇特、内涵最丰富的帝王陵墓之一。

这座豪华的地下宫殿里不仅有至今仍未挖掘的神秘地宫，还有已被发掘出的数千件兵马俑。秦始皇陵兵马俑为陶制，真人大小，神态各异，上施彩绘，体现了中国古代劳动人民的智慧和艺术创造力，也为研究秦代军事、文化和经济提供了丰富的实物资料。因此，秦始皇陵兵马俑的发掘被誉为"20世纪考古史上伟大的发现之一"。

本书分别从秦始皇、秦始皇陵、兵马俑和秦陵陪葬品四个方面解读秦陵与兵马俑，深入地介绍了这位帝王的生平、功绩与影响，展现了秦始皇陵的宏伟与神秘，展示了兵马俑与其他陪葬品的庞大与精致。现在，就让我们亲临骊山脚下渭水之滨的秦始皇陵，一层层地揭开它的神秘面纱。

expressions, are all wearing colored painting, which embody the wisdom and artistic creativity of Chinese people and also provide abundant material evidence for the study of military, culture and economy in the Qin Dynasty. Therefore, the excavation of the Mausoleum of Qin Shihuang and terracotta warriors is known as one of the greatest discoveries in the history of archaeology in the 20th century.

This book provides an in-depth introduction to the Mausoleum of Qin Shihuang and terracotta warriors from four aspects, namely the biography of Qin Shihuang and respective introductions to the imperial mausoleum, terracotta warriors and funeral objects, in order to let readers gain further understanding of this great emperor and his unprecedented achievements, as well as the grandeur and mystery of his mausoleum and the tremendous scale and delicate details of the terracotta army and other funeral objects. So, let us travel down to the foot of the Lishan Mountain, along the bank of Weihe River, all the way to the Mausoleum of Qin Shihuang to unveil its mystery and charm.

目录 Contents

秦始皇
Qin Shihuang 001

统一六国
Unifying the Other Six States 002

首称皇帝
The First Sovereign Emperor 006

北击匈奴、南征百越
Fighting Xiongnu in the North and
Baiyue in the South 014

始皇政绩
Qin Shihuang's Political Achievements 021

秦始皇陵
The Mausoleum of Qin Shihuang 035

皇陵的选址
Site Selection of the Imperial Mausoleum 036

皇陵的修建
Construction of the Imperial Mausoleum 040

皇陵的布局
Layout of the Imperial Mausoleum 045

皇陵的防盗体系
Security System of the Imperial Mausoleum .. 062

秦陵兵马俑
Terracotta Warriors in the Mausoleum of Qin Shihuang 069

偶然面世的奇迹
Emergence of Miracle 070

地下军阵
Underground Troops 074

各种兵俑
Various Figurines 087

秦陵中的其他陪葬品
Other Funeral Objects in the Mausoleum of Qin Shihuang 113

铜车马
Bronze Chariots and Horses 114

兵器
Ancient Weapon 123

铜水禽
Bronze Waterfowl 130

秦始皇
Qin Shihuang

　　秦始皇，姓嬴，名政，是中国历史上第一个大一统王朝——秦王朝的开国皇帝。公元前247年，年仅13岁的嬴政登上了秦国的王位。自公元前230年至公元前221年，秦王嬴政先后灭掉了韩、魏、楚、赵、燕、齐六个国家，完成了统一大业，建立起一个统一的多民族中央集权国家——秦。完成统一大业之后，秦始皇推行多项政策，例如书同文、车同轨和统一度量衡等，这些都对后世产生了极为深远的影响。公元前210年，秦始皇在东巡途中驾崩于沙丘（今河北省邢台境内），享年50岁。

Qin Shihuang (named Ying Zheng) the first emperor of the Qin Dynasty (221 B.C.-206 B.C.), founded the first unified empire in Chinese history. In 247 B.C., at the age of 13, Ying Zheng ascended the throne of State Qin. From 230 B.C. to 221 B.C., Ying Zheng conquered the other six states successively, namely Han, Wei, Chu, Zhao, Yan and Qi, and accomplished the great cause of unification. Ying Zheng constructed a unified and centralized multi-ethnic empire—the Qin Dynasty (221 B.C.-206 B.C.). After the unification, Qin Shihuang (Ying Zheng) implemented many policies: he standardized the Chinese characters, units of measurements and the national transport system, which have exerted an extensive and profound influence on future generations. He has a far-reaching and significant effect on both China and the rest of the world. In 210 B.C., Qin Shihuang died at the age of 50 in Shaqiu (now Xingtai City, Hebei Province) during his tour to eastern China.

> 统一六国

战国（前475—前221）时代是中国历史上最为动荡的时期之一。周王朝的权势被进一步削弱，各方诸侯之间的攻伐战争不断。在黄河和长江两大流域的广袤土地上，齐、楚、燕、韩、赵、魏、秦七个诸侯国为争夺霸权发生的战争从未停止过。战争的规模和作战方式也在不断变化，步兵、骑兵和弓弩兵逐渐成为作战的主力，而在作战的实力和技巧上，秦国逐渐占据优势地位。

秦王嬴政亲政之后，凭借着前代的积累，国力达到了鼎盛。嬴政开始了吞并六国、统一天下的计划。在此时，虽然秦国的军事力量比任何一个诸侯国的力量都要强大，但同时要面临其他六国的"同

> Unifying the Other Six States

The end of the Warring States Period is one of the most turbulent periods in Chinese history. The power and influence of the Eastern Zhou Dynasty (770 B.C.-256 B.C.) was further crippled and the wars among different states continued constantly. In the vast areas along the Yangtze River and Yellow River, the wars for supremacy among the seven powerful states Qi, Chu, Yan, Han, Zhao, Wei and Qin occurred frequently. The scales and operational modes of the wars varied continuously as well. The infantry, cavalry and crossbowman gradually became the principal force. And in terms of the strength and tactical skill in the battle, State Qin gradually dominated its rivals.

When Ying Zheng, the King of State Qin, was in power, State Qin reached its heyday with the previous accumulation of

• 秦始皇画像
Portrait of Qin Shihuang

仇敌忾", 而以秦朝的国力是不能与联合起来的六国相抗衡的。此时, 嬴政展示出一位杰出战略家的智慧, 采用了"远交齐燕, 近攻赵韩"的攻略, 防止六国联合。

公元前236年, 嬴政派秦国大将王翦和杨端和率30万秦军进攻赵国, 利用优势兵力迅速占领了上党郡（今山西省东南部）及河间地区。公元前234年, 秦军又攻下赵国的几座重要城池, 赵国军队阵亡10余万人。公元前228年, 秦军攻克了

wealth. Ying Zheng began to implement his plan of conquering the other six states and unifying the country. Although the military force of Qin exceeded that of any other states at that time, it had to face the situation of "the sharing hatred towards the same enemy" of the rest six states at the same time. Since Qin's power could not rival the united strength of the other six states. Therefore, Ying Zheng demonstrated his talent as an outstanding strategist and employed the tactic of "befriending the distant Qi and Yan while attacking the nearby Zhao and Han", in order to prevent the other six states from forming an alliance.

In 236 B.C., Ying Zheng instructed two military generals Wang Jian and Yang Duanhe to command 300,000 Qin's soldiers to attack State Zhao. Depending on the advantage of superior military strength, Qin's troop took Shangdang County (now in the southeast of Shanxi Province) and Hejian region. In 234 B.C, the Qin's troop seized several other important cities of State Zhao and killed more than 100,000 Zhao's soldiers. In 228 B.C., the Qin's troop captured the capitial city of State Zhao, Handan.

The weaker State Wei and State Yan were destroyed soon. The largest

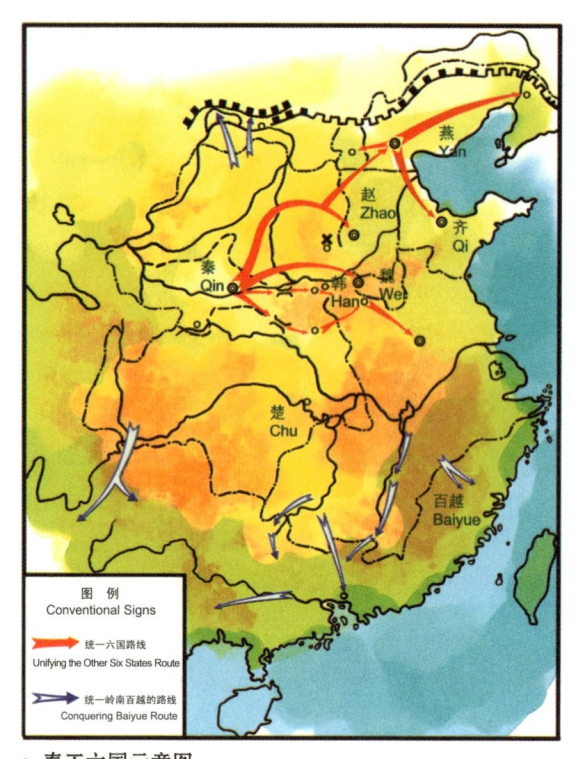

● 秦灭六国示意图
Map of Qin's Conquest of the Other Six States

赵国都城邯郸。

弱小的魏国和燕国很快被秦所灭。此时，秦国面临的最大敌人便是齐、楚。从齐、楚两国的实力比较来看，楚远比齐强大，齐国军力虽然相对较弱，但国力雄厚。如若先攻齐，免不了要和较强大的楚同时发生恶战，而且秦国还很有可能遭受齐、楚两军的夹击。有鉴于

enemies faced by State Qin were State Qi and State Chu at that moment. Comparing the military strength of these two states, it was clear that State Chu was far more powerful than State Qi. However, Qi was weak in military but abundant in national wealth. Therefore, it would be inevitable to fall into an arduous battle with both states at the same time if the Qin's troop attacked State Qi first; in addition, it was highly possible for State Qin to be confronted with the converging attack of the Qi and Chu's troops. Given the possibility, Ying Zheng adopted the tactic of "focusing main force on main enemy", namely launching assault on State Chu.

In 225 B.C., the commander Li Xin led 200,000 Qin's troop to attack State Chu under the order of Qin Shihuang but was defeated. In 224 B.C., Wang Jian was appointed to command 600,000 troops to assault State Chu. Learning the lesson from the failure of Li Xin who "underestimated the enemy and proceeded rashly", Wang

此，嬴政便采取了"集中主力打击主要敌人"的战略——攻楚。

公元前225年，秦始皇派大将李信率20万秦兵伐楚，旋即兵败。公元前224年，嬴政改派王翦率领60万大军伐楚。王翦吸取了李信"轻敌冒进"导致失败的教训，坚守营盘拒不出战。在营寨里面的秦军养精蓄锐、积蓄斗志。公元前223年，时机成熟，秦军犹如野兽般冲入楚营。楚军大败，楚国灭亡。

楚亡之后，齐国独木难支，一战即溃。齐国也灭亡了。

公元前221年，秦王嬴政完成了自己的统一大业，中国历史掀开了新的篇章。

Jian and his troops were stationed in the military camps persistently and refused to march army for battle. Within the barracks, the Qin's troop conserved their strength. Then, while the time was right, Qin's troop organized an assault on Chu's army and won the whole battle. State Chu was destroyed.

It was difficult for State Qi to protect and support itself alone after State Chu perished. State Qi was conquered after only one battle with State Qin.

In 221 B.C., Ying Zheng, the King of State Qin accomplished the great undertaking of China's unification, which opened a new chapter of Chinese history.

- 透雕云纹戈（战国）
Dagger-axe Enchased with Cloud Pattern (Warring States Period, 475 B.C.-221 B.C.)

- 双环首云纹铜剑（战国）
Bronze Sword with Cloud Pattern and a Two-ring Hilt (Warring States Period, 475 B.C.-221 B.C.)

> 首称皇帝

春秋战国时期，诸侯国的最高统治者被称为"君"或"王"。到了战国后期，秦国和齐国的君主曾一度称"帝"。

一统天下之后，嬴政以为过去的"君""王""帝"等称号都不足以显示自己的尊崇地位和伟大功绩，便根据"三皇五帝"（远古时期帝王的简称）创造出了"皇帝"这个新头衔，寓意自己"德兼三皇，功高五帝"。从秦朝嬴政开始，"皇帝"这个尊号便成为中国封建社会最高统治者的称谓，延续了2000多年。嬴政做了中国历史上第一个皇帝。为了维持千朝万代的家族统治，秦始皇还规定：自己死后，皇位传给子孙时后继者沿称"二世皇帝""三世皇帝"……以

> The First Sovereign Emperor

During the Spring and Autumn Period and Warring States Period, rulers of the states were titled *Jun* (chief) or *Wang* (king). In the late Warring States Period, the leaders of State Qin and State Qi once proclaimed themselves as *Di* (emperor).

After the unification of China, Ying Zheng believed that the previous *Jun*, *Wang* and *Di* could not represent his distinguished status and outstanding contributions. According to the Three Sovereigns and Five Emperors (*Sanhuang Wudi*, titles of mythological rulers in ancient times), Ying Zheng invented a new title for himself as *Huangdi* (sovereign emperor), meaning that his virtues and contributions could be compared with or even exceed that of the Three Sovereigns and Five Emperors. From then on, the honorific title *Huangdi* was succeeded by the highest rulers in

秦代舞蹈
Dance of the Qin Dynasty

至万世不休。

"皇帝"称谓的出现，反映了一种新的统治观念的产生。"皇"和"帝"两个字结合起来，意指君权神授。皇帝尊崇的地位是上天给予的，天地是万物之主，而皇帝自己则是代表天地来行使人世间的统治权。借"皇帝"的称号，秦始皇神化了自己的君权。

为了彰显"君权神授"，秦始皇又采取了一系列"尊君"的措施，如天子自称为"朕"。"朕"

Chinese feudal society afterwards for more than 2,000 years. Ying Zheng became the first emperor in Chinese history. For the longevity of his family's domination, Qin Shihuang instructed that the successors who would inherit the throne should continue to use titles like *Huangdi* II and *Huangdi* III generation after generation after his death.

The occurrence of the title *Huangdi* reflects the birth of a new ruling concept. The combination of *Huang* (sovereign) and *Di* (emperor) by Qin Shihuang refers to the emperor's divine right. The

三皇五帝

三皇五帝是传说中的远古帝王。三皇是中国早期的三个帝王，一般认为是燧人、伏羲和神农。他们分别代表了三个时代：燧人氏代表文明启蒙时期，伏羲代表文明时代和神农氏代表农耕时代。这三个时期历史久远，相当于三个朝代，时间跨度至少有几千年之久。五帝是神农氏之后、夏禹之前出现的五个帝王，一般认为是黄帝、颛顼、帝喾、唐尧和虞舜。他们属于一个独立的朝代，其时间跨度四五百年，距今约4000多年。

Three Sovereigns and Five Emperors

Three Sovereigns and Five Emperors are rulers in ancient time in China. Three Sovereigns refers to the three emperors in early Chinese history, generally known as Suiren, Fuxi and Shennong. These also mean three respective ages in ancient times, namely Suiren is on behalf of the enlightenment of civilization, Fuxi the age of civilization and Shennong the age of agriculture. Five Emperors emerged after Shennong's but before Xiayu's appearance, normally indicating Emperor Huang, Zhuanxu, Diku (Emperor Ku), Tangyao (Emperor Yao) and Yushun (Emperor Shun). They belonged to different independent dynasties with a time span of approximately 400 to 500 years, about more than 4,000 years ago.

honorable position of the emperor was granted by the heaven, which is to say that the emperor represents the heaven and earth to execute the right of ruling the world. Qin Shihuang deified his power by entitling himself as *Huangdi*.

In order to demonstrate his divine right as the emperor, Qin Shihuang implemented a series of measures, including calling himself *Zhen*. The meaning of *Zhen* is I or me, which could be used by normal people previously. However, from then on, *Zhen* could be exclusively used by the emperor. Additionally, the reference to the Emperor's name in writing was forbidden and tabooed. In the official documents, whenever the word *Huangdi* appeared, it should be written on a new line without leaving space at the beginning. The purpose of implementing these rules was to highlight the special position of the emperor and his imperial family, stress the difference of the emperor from the normal public and strengthen the authority of imperial power in people's mind.

To govern the country effectively, based on the experience of arranging and setting up official positions in the Warring States Period (475 B.C.-221 B.C.), Qin Shihuang established a relatively

字的意义与"我"相同，以前一般人也可以使用，但自秦始皇开始，只限定皇帝专用。此外，在文字中不能提及皇帝的名字，要避讳。书写的文件上逢"皇帝"等字句时，都要另起一行来顶格书写。这些规定，目的在于突出天子的特殊地位，强调皇帝与众不同，强化皇权在人们心中的权威感。

为了有效地管理国家，秦始皇 integrated feudal centralized system and administrative organization. Furthermore, drawing lessons from the tangled warfare and the separation situation during the Spring and Autumn Period and Warring States Period (770 B.C. - 221 B.C.), Qin Shihuang abolished the system of enfeoffment at the local level and implemented the system of prefectures and counties. He divided the country into 36 counties and later added to 41.

- "酉阳丞印"封泥（秦代）

秦始皇在中央设丞相、太尉、御史大夫。丞相有两位，为百官之首，掌政事；太尉掌军事；御史大夫掌图籍秘书（地图和户口册等），负责监察百官，并协助丞相处理政务。丞相、太尉、御史大夫以下是分掌具体行政事务的主管官员。丞相、太尉、御史大夫连同大臣们讨论政务，提供可行性方案，最终由皇帝做裁决。

Sealing Clay of "Youyang Assistant Officer's Seal" (Qin Dynasty, 221 B.C.-206 B.C.)

In the central government, Qin Shihuang nominated Chengxiang (counselors-in-chief), Taiwei (minister of war) and Yushi Dafu (censor-in-chief). There were two counselors-in-chief as the heads of all officials whose main task was to deal with governmental affairs; the minister of war was responsible for the military affairs; the censor-in-chief was in charge of maps, books and household register as well as the supervision of all officials and provided assistance to the counselor-in-chief. Below the counselor-in-chief, minister of war and censor-in-chief, there were several officers-in-charge whose main job included the concrete administrative affairs. The counselor-in-chief, minister of war, censor-in-chief and other major officials should conduct discussions on the governmental affairs and based on that, worked out feasible plans for the emperor to decide.

- **《阿房宫图》（清 袁耀）**

  阿房宫修建于秦始皇三十五年（前212后）。秦始皇统一全国以后，在都城咸阳大兴土木，建宫筑殿，其中所建宫殿中规模最大的就是阿房宫。

  Epang Palace, by Yuan Yao (Qing Dynasty, 1616-1911)

  The Epang Palace was built in the 35th year of Qin Shihuang's reign (212 B.C.). After the unification, Qin Shihuang built several palaces in the capital city Xianyang, among which the Epang Palace was the broadest in scale.

吸取了战国时期设置官职的经验，建立了一套相对完整的中央集权制度和行政机构。此外，秦始皇总结了春秋战国时期各地诸侯混战、割据的教训，废除了前代的分封制，改行郡县制。他把治下的国家分成三十六郡，以后又陆续增设至四十一郡。

秦始皇泰山封禅

秦始皇二十八年（前219年），即统一六国后的第三年，秦始皇东巡郡县，来到泰山举行封禅大典，以表明自己当上皇帝是受命于天的。封禅是中国古已有之的礼仪，"封"为祭天，"禅"为祭地，封禅即中国古代帝王在太平盛世或天降祥瑞之时祭祀天地的大型典礼。古人认为，群山之中以泰山最为高大雄伟，且位居中原地区，为"天下第一山"，因此人间的帝王到泰山去祭拜过天帝后，才算受命于天。秦始皇登基后，也"顺应天理"，劈山修路，登上泰山之顶行封礼，并刻石以歌功颂德。

Qin Shihuang's Sacrificial Ceremony on Taishan Mountain

In the 28th year of the reign of Qin Shihuang (219 B.C.), the 3rd year after unifying the other six states, Qin Shihuang held the imperial sacrificial ceremony on Taishan Mountain on his tour to eastern China in order to demonstrate that his status was granted by the heaven. This traditional sacrificial ceremony had long existed in ancient China while *Feng* refers to sacrifice to heaven and *Shan* refers to sacrifice to earth, and *Fengshan* is an important and grand ceremony held by emperors in ancient China when it was in the time of peace and prosperity or there

- 泰山

泰山位于山东泰安与济南之间，自然景观雄伟，于1987年被列入《世界遗产名录》。数千年来，先后有十二位皇帝来到泰山封禅。

Taishan Mountain

Taishan Mountain is located between Tai'an City and Jinan City, Shandong Province with magnificent natural sceneries. It has been listed in the UNESCO World Heritage List since 1987. Totally 12 emperors held the sacrificial ceremonies on Taishan Mountain in the past thousands of years.

were auspicious signs. Ancient Chinese people believed that Taishan Mountain was the most magnificent mountain among all and located in Central China, known as the Greatest Mountain in the World. Therefore, the emperor was regarded to have received the instructions and divine right from the heaven after this sacrificial ceremony on Taishan Mountain. After ascending the throne, Qin Shihuang complied with the heaven's instruction to administer the mountain, construct new roads, host the sacrificial ceremony on the top of Taishan Mountain and inscribe his achievements and virtues into the stones for people to praise.

• 秦泰山石刻
Stone Inscription in Taishan Mountain (Qin Dynasty, 221 B.C.-206 B.C.)

传国玉玺

传国玉玺是中国古代皇帝的信物，富有神秘的色彩。相传，秦始皇统一中国后，命令能工巧匠将和氏璧雕琢成传国玉玺，并且命丞相李斯在和氏璧上篆刻"受命于天，既寿永昌"八个篆字。玉玺成为秦始皇权力的象征。

此后，传国玉玺成为历代王朝正统的象征。历代帝王都将传国玉玺奉若奇珍，当成国之重器加以保存和收藏。帝王要是能得到传国玉玺，就意味着自己"受命于天"，失去了它则表示"气数已尽"。这枚传国玉玺后来屡易其主，被你争我夺，最终销声匿迹。

• 定陵出土的神宗皇帝谥宝（明）
Imperial Jade Seal of Emperor Shenzong of the Ming Dynasty Unearthed from Dingling Mausoleum

Imperial Jade Seal

The imperial jade seal represents the kingship in ancient China, tinted with a mystical color. According to legend, after unifying China, Qin Shihuang instructed skillful craftsmen to carve a jade into the imperial jade seal and asked prime minister Li Si to carve 8 Chinese characters onto the seal whose meaning is "Mandate Granted by Heaven, For Longevity and Prosperity". This jade seal became the symbol of Qin Shihuang's power and authority.

From then on, the imperial jade seal was regarded as the symbol of orthodox regime. Emperors considered the jade seal as the national treasure and preserved it carefully and seriously as obtaining the seal means the emperor masters the divine power from heaven while losing it means the end of fate. The owner of this jade seal changed repeatedly afterwards and aroused furious fights. In the end, this legendary jade seal disappeared.

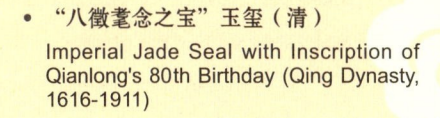

• "八徵耄念之宝"玉玺（清）
Imperial Jade Seal with Inscription of Qianlong's 80th Birthday (Qing Dynasty, 1616-1911)

> 北击匈奴、南征百越

嬴政灭六国，实现了中原地区的统一，但这并未标志着秦军的征战已经结束。

匈奴是一个历史悠久的北方游牧民族，由弱到强。匈奴人乘秦灭六国无暇顾及北方之机，在首领大单于的带领下，攻占了北方的广阔地区。秦国的都城咸阳（今陕西省咸阳市）面临严重威胁。

与此同时，地处五岭之南的百越也逐渐强大起来。百越是中国古代南方少数民族越人的总称，分布在今浙江、福建、广东、广西、云南等地。在春秋战国时期，百越就曾多次与中原诸国交战。因此，百越对秦的统一和政治的稳定同样造成了一定的威胁。

为了使统治长治久安，秦朝

> Fighting Xiongnu in the North and Baiyue in the South

Although Ying Zheng conquered the other six states and unified Central China, this did not terminate the military operation of Qin's troop.

With a long history, Xiongnu inhabited in north China as a nomadic tribe and gradually developed and expanded their sphere of power and influence. Under the leadership of Chief Chanyu (leader), Xiongnu tribe attacked and captured large areas of northern China while State Qin concentrated on attacking the other six states. Therefore, the capital city of State Qin, Xianyang (now Xianyang City, Shaanxi Province) was faced with grave threats.

At the same time, Baiyue, located in the south of the Five Ridges (Lingnan), became increasingly powerful. It denoted

• 《胡人出猎图》（明 张龙章）
Hunting in Northern Tribes, by Zhang Longzhang (Ming Dynasty, 1368-1644)

必须对这两股政治军事势力给予打击和征服。相比较而言，匈奴的势力较百越更强，于是秦始皇采用了"先弱后强、先远后近"的征战方针，决定首先平定南越。

公元前218年，50万秦军发动了征服岭南越人的战争，双方对峙达三年之久。在对峙过程中，秦军的兵力补充和粮草供给困难。为了

the ethnic groups inhabiting in the south of ancient China, with the distribution areas covering Zhejiang, Fujian, Guangdong, Guangxi and Yunnan at present. During the Spring and Autumn Period and Warring States Period (770 B.C. - 221 B.C.), Baiyue conducted several battles with the states in Central China. Therefore, Baiyue posed threats to the unification and political stability of Qin.

灵渠

　　灵渠是世界上最古老的运河之一，有"世界古代水利建筑明珠"的美誉。它位于广西壮族自治区兴安县境内，于公元前214年凿成通航，全长37.4公里，设计科学、建筑精巧，沟通了长江和珠江两大水系，自古就是中国岭南与中原地区之间的水路交通要道，至今仍对航运、农田灌溉起着重要作用。

Lingqu Canal

As one of the oldest canals in the world, Lingqu Canal enjoys the reputation of the "Pearl of the Ancient Water Conservancy Projects in the World". Located in Xing'an County, Guangxi Zhuang Autonomous Region and opened to navigation in 214 B.C., Lingqu Canal has a total length of 37.4 kilometres, with scientific design and delicate structure, and links the Yangtze River and the Pearl River. From the ancient time, it has long been an important waterway connecting Lingnan and Central China. Until now, it has still played an indispensable role in shipping and irrigation.

• 广西桂林灵渠 (图片提供：全景正片)
Lingqu Canal in Guilin City, Guangxi

扭转战略颓势，秦始皇决意开凿灵渠。公元前217年，秦始皇命监御史史禄在今广西兴安县境内开凿灵渠。灵渠沟通了长江和珠江水系。如此一来，秦军的粮饷就能络绎不绝地运到岭南前线，攻越的秦军将士得到了可靠的物质保障。

公元前214年，秦军再次进攻百越各部族，旋即击溃敌军防线，整个岭南地区从此划入了秦朝的版图。

为了保持岭南的稳定，秦始皇命进军岭南的将士留守当地"屯戍"。这支生力军农忙时耕种土地，以解决粮草问题；农闲时进行操练，保持军队战斗力。亦兵亦农的秦军为维护岭南的稳定提供了有力的保障。此外，秦始皇从中原向岭南地区大批移民。屯兵和移民与当地的越人共同生活、通婚、繁衍后代，安定了岭南。

征服百越之后，秦始皇派大将蒙恬率30万大军攻打匈奴，由战略防御转为战略进攻。匈奴不断失利，被迫向北迁徙。此举暂时解除了匈奴对秦北方领土的威胁，使今河套内外的广大地区在一个相当长的时期内摆脱了兵难。为巩固胜

In order to maintain the prosperity and stability of Qin's governance, it was necessary to crack down and conquer these two military and political forces. Compared with Baiyue, Xiongnu was a more powerful enemy and based on that, Qin Shihuang decided to suppress Nanyue (an ancient kingdom belonged to Baiyue) first as the strategy of "dealing with the weak and remote followed by the strong and nearby".

In 218 B.C., 500,000 Qin's troop waged war against Yue and this war lasted as long as 3 years. During this process, affected by the serious problems of supply of military forces and army provisions and in order to reverse the unfavorable situation, Qin Shihuang resolved to excavate Lingqu Canal. In 217 B.C., Qin Shihuang ordered official censor Shi Lu to begin the project of constructing Lingqu Canal in Xing'an County in present Guangxi. Lingqu Canal links the Yangtze River and the Pearl River. Thus, the provisions as well as funds of troops could be transported to the Lingnan frontline smoothly and continuously, which reliably guaranteed the supply of goods and materials to Qin's troop.

In 214 B.C., Qin's troop attacked

Baiyue again and defeated their defense. The whole Lingnan region became a part of Qin's territory.

To stabilize Lingnan, Qin Shihuang instructed officers and soldiers who defeated Lingnan to stay and garrison that region. This group of people cultivated land to supply army provisions in farming season; for the rest of time, they conducted military drills in order to retain the fighting capacity. Performed both as farmers and soldiers, they proved to an effective force to stabilize Lingnan region. Furthermore, Qin Shihuang introduced large quantities of people from Central China to Lingnan region. Soldiers who garrisoned Lingnan and migratory people lived together with the local people of Yue people through marriages and other ways for generations, bringing peace and stability to Lingnan.

After conquering Baiyue, Qin Shihuang ordered famous army general Meng Tian to lead 300,000 Qin's soldiers to attack Xiongnu tribe, as the turning point of defensive to offensive. Xiongnu suffered from military setback and was forced to move to the north, which temporarily removed this threat to Qin and made the vast area at the bend of Yellow River free from the

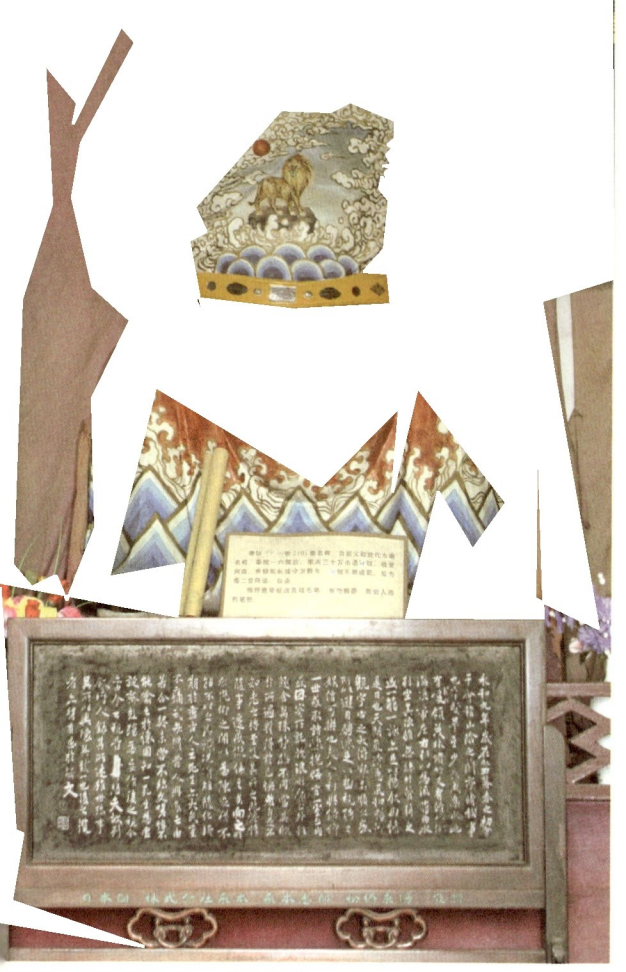

- 蒙恬塑像

蒙恬（？—前210），秦始皇时期的著名将领，也是中国西北最早的开发者。

Statue of Meng Tian

Meng Tian (?-210 B.C.), was famous as a Qin's military general and known as the earliest developer of the northwest China.

● 秦代铜镞（兵器）
Bronze Arrowheads (Ancient Weapon) (Qin Dynasty, 221 B.C.-206 B.C.)

利果实，秦始皇在此地设置了九原郡。同时为了防止匈奴南下扰边，蒙恬奉秦始皇命令征发大量的民工在原燕国、赵国和秦国长城的基础上，修筑了西起临洮（今甘肃岷县）、东到辽东的长城。

秦始皇南征百越；北击匈奴，夺回河套地区。此外，秦始皇还开通了往西南的五尺道（大致自今四川宜宾至云南曲靖一线），

disaster of war for a considerably long period of time. In order to consolidate this situation, Qin Shihuang established Jiuyuan County here. What is more, to prevent Xiongnu's harassment, based on the Great Walls within previous States Yan, Zhao and Qin, Meng Tian collected large numbers of laborers to expand the previous Great Walls and constructed a new part stretching from Lintao County in the west (now Minxian County, Gansu Province) to the Great Wall in the

控制了当地的部族，将政治势力伸入云贵高原。秦始皇由此奠定了中国版图的大致轮廓，使形成了一个统一的多民族的大国。

southeast part of Liaoning Province in the east.

In the south, Qin Shihuang conquered Baiyue; in the north, he defeated Xiongnu and recaptured the bend region of Yellow River. Additionally, Qin Shihuang constructed the Wuchi Road to the southwest (now from Yibin City of Sichuan Province to Qujing City of Yunnan Province generally), controlled the local tribes and made his political influence permeate into the Yunnan-Guizhou Plateau. From then on, Qin Shihuang had finished drawing the general outline of Chinese territory and established a unified and multi-ethnic empire.

> 始皇政绩

秦始皇是中国历史上有作为的皇帝之一。他不仅完成了中国陆地疆域的大一统，还在文化上实现了文字的统一，并且还统一了钱币，统一了度量衡，统一了车轨……为其后各朝代谋求统一奠定了基础。

书同文

春秋战国时期的文字存在着区域差异，几个主要的诸侯国都有自己的语言文字。秦始皇统一中原后，这种状况不但妨碍了各地之间的交流，也影响了政策法令的推行。于是，秦始皇下令丞相李斯等人着手进行文字的整理和统一工作。

李斯以秦国通用的大篆为基础，吸取齐鲁等地通行的"蝌蚪

> Qin Shihuang's Political Achievements

Qin Shihuang is one of the most capable and outstanding imperial emperors in Chinese history. Not limited to initially unify Chinese land territory, he also standardized Chinese characters in cultural area, currency, units of measurements and the length of cart axles's spacing, which laid foundation of the unification of the following dynasties.

Standardizing Chinese Characters

In the Spring and Autumn Period and Warring States Period (770 B.C. - 221 B.C.), Chinese characters varied from region to region and major states owned their unique languages and characters. After unifying Central China, that circumstance hindered the communication of different areas and affected the implementation of

• 秦代竹简

竹简是战国至魏晋时代的书写材料。造纸术发明之后，竹简逐渐退出历史舞台。

Bamboo Slip of the Qin Dynasty (221 B.C.-206 B.C.)

The bamboo slip is a kind of writing material employed from the Warring States Period (475 B.C.-221 B.C.) to the Wei Dynasty (220-265) and the Jin Dynasty (265-420). After the emergence of papermaking technology, bamboo slips gradually stepped down from the stage of history.

文"笔画简洁的优点，创造出一种形体圆融齐整、笔画简洁的新文字。这种统一的新文字被称为"秦篆"，又称"小篆"。秦始皇将其作为秦朝官方规范的文字在全国强令推广，同时废除其他异体字，这就是"书同文"。

秦始皇在"书同文"的过程中，命令李斯创立小篆后，又采

unified policies and laws. Based on this situation, therefore, Qin Shihuang ordered his prime minister Li Si and other officers to deal with this problem.

Based on the universal large seal script in State Qin while absorbing the advantage of "tadpole script" prevailing in Qilu region (now Shandong Province) because of its concise strokes, a harmonious, neat and succinctly designed new script was invented. This new unified script is known

纳了程邈整理的隶书。隶书也叫"隶字""古书",是在篆书基础上,为适应书写便捷的需要产生的字体。隶书是将小篆加以简化,把小篆匀圆的线条变成平直方正的笔画,更便于书写。小篆和隶书实际上是两个系统,代表着汉字发展的两大阶段。小篆是象形体古文字的结束,隶书是改象形为笔画化的新文字的开始。

as Qin's seal script or small seal script and was popularized in national scale as the official normative characters while other characters were abolished, called as standardizing the Chinese characters in history.

During the reform process, besides the small seal script invented by Li Si, Qin Shihuang also adopted the clerical script proposed by Cheng Miao. The clerical script is also known as clerical character or archaic script, developed from the seal script in order to facilitate writing. The clerical script is from the simplified small seal script, where the soft and curving strokes are replaced by straight and square ones, making it convenient to write. However, these two scripts are two different systems, marking two phases of Chinese characters' development. The small seal script puts an end to the hieroglyphic and the clerical script is the beginning of a new style of characters which concentrates on the strokes.

As a great conclusion of the development and evolvement of ancient Chinese characters, the magnificent undertaking of standardizing and simplifying Chinese characters made by Qin Shihuang is also a major reform of writing system. It positively promotes the

• 秦代木牍
Wooden Tablet (Qin Dynasty, 221 B.C.-206 B.C.)

- "皇"字（隶书）
  Chinese Character "*Huang* (Emperor)" (Clerical Script)

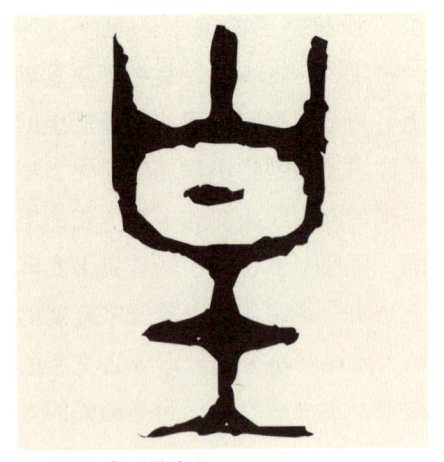

- "皇"字（篆书）
  Chinese Character "*Huang* (Emperor)" (Seal Script)

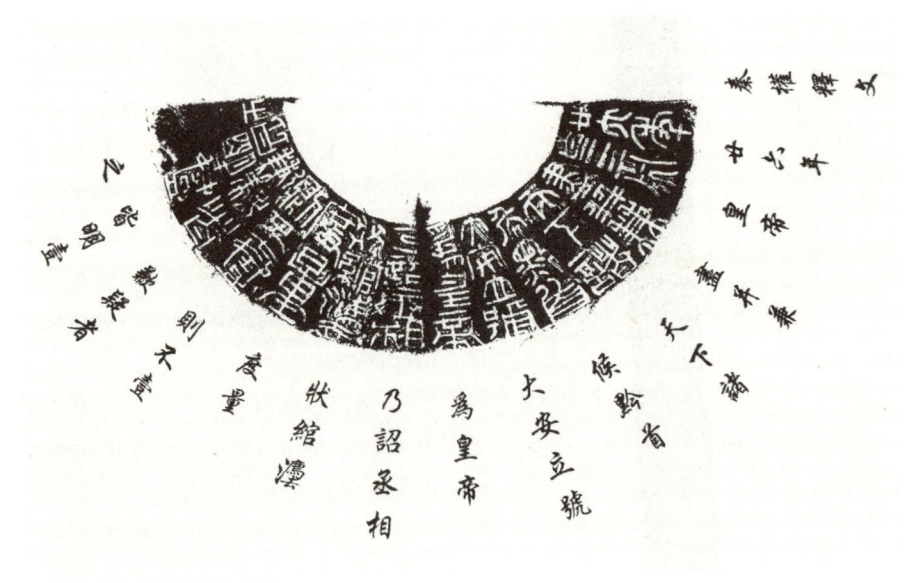

- 秦代"始皇诏铜权"铭文
  Inscription on "Imperial Bronze Weight Inscribed with the Edict of Qin Shihuang" (Qin Dynasty, 221 B.C.-206 B.C.)

秦始皇下令统一和简化文字，是对中国古代文字发展、演变的一次总结，也是一次大的文字改革，对中国文化的交流发展、维护国家统一局面起到了积极的作用。

度同制

春秋战国时期，各国的度量衡制度不一致。秦统一后，以原秦国的度、量、衡为单位标准，淘汰了与此不合的制度，史称"度同制"。秦在原标准器上加刻诏书铭文，或另行制作相同的标准器，刻上铭文，发放至全国。为了保障"度同制"的实施，秦始皇明令：凡与标准不同的度、量、衡一律禁

communication, development of Chinese culture as well as unification maintenance.

Standardizing Units of Measurements

In the Spring and Autumn Period and Warring States Period (770 B.C. - 221 B.C.), the measurements of each states were different. After Qin unified China, the previous standards of length, capacity and weight prevailed in State Qin were adopted and other measurements were eliminated, known as "standardizing units of measurements" in history. The previous standard measuring implements were carved with imperial edicts or imperial inscriptions, and the same new measuring implements were produced with inscriptions which were popularized

- **秦代铜方升（量器）**

铜方升是古代的一种量器，即铜制的升。此方升长18.7厘米，深2.51厘米，内口长12.47厘米，宽6.897厘米，容积为1升（合今0.001立方米）。

Bronze Square *Sheng* (Measuring Vessel) (Qin Dynasty, 221 B.C.-206 B.C.)

The bronze square *Sheng* is an ancient measuring vessel, namely a measurement vessel made out of bronze. The square *Sheng* is 18.7 centimetres long and 2.51 centimetres deep with its internal opening 12.47 centimetres long and 6.897 centimetres wide. Its total volume is 1 liter (approximately 0.001 cubic meter).

• 秦代铜权

铜权是古代的一种衡器，相当于现在的秤砣。

Bronze Weight (Qin Dynasty, 221 B.C.-206 B.C.)

The bronze weight is an ancient weighing apparatus whose function is similar to the present weight poise.

止使用。此外在田制上，秦王朝还规定6尺（约合今230厘米）为一步，1步×240步为一亩。这一亩制以后沿用千年而不变。

改良币制

春秋战国时期，各诸侯国的货币制度不一致，严重影响了各国的经济交流。统一中原之后，秦始皇采取了两种统一货币的方法：一是由国家统一铸币，严惩私人铸币，将货币的制造权牢牢掌握在国家手中；二是统一通行两种货币，即上币黄金和下币铜钱。改黄金以"镒"为单位，一镒为二十两；铜钱以"半两"为单位，并明确铸币铭"半两"二字。秦朝铜钱造型为

to every corner of the country. To ensure the implementation of new units of measurements, Qin Shihuang instructed that all units of measures which were not up to this standard should be forbidden. In terms of the field system, according to the regulation of Qin, 6 *Chi* (approximately 230 centimetres) equals to 1 *Bu* and 1 *Bu* times 240 *Bu* equals to 1 *Mu* (approximately 666.7 square meters). This measurement system was inherited by the following dynasties and lasted for thousands of years.

Reforming Currency System

In the Spring and Autumn Period and Warring States Period (770 B.C. - 221 B.C.), states employed very different currency systems and this affected the economic exchange of each state.

战国时期其他诸侯国的钱币
Currencies of Other States during Warring States Period (475 B.C.-221 B.C.)

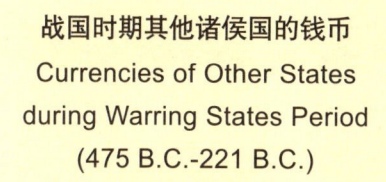

• 楚国的蚁鼻钱
Yibi (literally means ant on the nose) Coin of State Chu

• 魏国的釿布币
Round Feet Spade-shaped Coin of State Wei

• 齐国的刀币
Knife-shaped Coin of State Qi

After the unification of Central China, Qin Shihuang adopted two methods to standardize the currency: one was that the country coined the currency uniformly and gave punishment to those private coiners. Through this method, the currency manufacturing right was tightly held by the nation. The second method was to standardize the two existing currencies, namely the gold and bronze coins. The unit of gold was changed to *Yi* and 1 *Yi* equals 20 *Liang*; the bronze coins used *Banliang* as the unit and the characters *Ban* and *Liang* were inscribed on the coins. The bronze coins of the Qin Dynasty are designed as round coin with square hole, also called as Qin's *Banliang* coin. Pearls, jades, tortoise shells, silver and tin coins used to be currencies in the other six states could not be used any more.

Compared with the currency in other states in the Warring States Period (475 B.C.-221 B.C.), *Banliang* coins were easy to carry and they could be clustered together and fastened around people's waists, ensuring safety and convenience. The word *Panchan* (travelling expense, *Pan* and *Chan* mean wraping around) is sourced from here.

In the more than two thousand years after the Qin Dynasty (221 B.C.-206 B.C.),

• 秦代圆形方孔钱
Round Coin with Square Hole (Qin Dynasty, 221 B.C.-206 B.C.)

圆形方孔，俗称"秦半两"。原来六国通行的珠玉、龟贝、银锡等予以废止，不得再充当货币。

相对于战国时期其他诸侯国的钱币，秦朝的圆形方孔钱携带方便：把铜钱盘起来缠绕腰间，既方便携带又安全。"盘缠"一词便来源于此。

秦朝以后两千多年间的钱币，除东汉王莽一度行刀币、布币外，中间都有一方孔，故称钱为"方孔钱"。

整治交通和车同轨

从公元前222年开始，为了调兵、纳粮和发展经济，秦始皇开始修筑以国都咸阳为中心、通往八方

except for the knife-shaped coin circulated under Wang Mang's new currency system, ancient Chinese coins are designed with a square hole in the middle known as square hole coins.

Standardizing Transport System and Length of Cart Axles

Since 222 B.C., Qin Shihuang began to construct imperial highways from the capital city Xianyang as the center to all directions for the purposes of troop movement, grain collection and economic development. The imperial highway obtains a variety of functions: on the one hand, it facilitated the transportation of different regions and made contributions to the emperor's control of the areas that used to be the six states; on the other hand,

的驰道，类似于现代的高速公路。驰道的作用有很多。一方面是方便了各地的交通，利于秦始皇管理六国旧地；另一方面，驰道方便了战争前线的粮草和兵员补给，有力保障了战争的胜利。秦朝的驰道，除秦直道和秦栈道外，大多在秦故地、六国旧道以及在秦征伐六国时修建道路的基础上改造而成。

秦始皇统一中原之前，各诸侯国向来是没有统一的交通制度的，各地的车辆大小也不一样，因此车道也有宽有窄。秦统一六国后，规

this highway provided convenience to the supply of army provisions and soldiers and reliably ensured the victory of war. Except the straight roads and plank roads of Qin, the majority of imperial highways of Qin were reconstructed on roads in State Qin and other six states as well as ones for wars with other states.

Before Central China was unified, the states did not share the same transportation system. The sizes of carts in each region varied, leading to the differences existing in the width of roads. After the unification, the length of the cart axle was determined in 6 *Chi*, making the wheel axle the same

- 战国青铜车辕饰
Bronze Ornaments of Cart Shaft (Warring States Period, 475 B.C.-221 B.C.)

定车辆上两个轮子的距离一律为六尺，使车轮的轨道相同。这样，全国各地车辆陆路往来就方便很多了，史称"车同轨"。

for all carts. Therefore, the transportation of different regions became more convenient, known as "standardizing length of cart axles".

修筑长城

长城是古代中国在不同时期内，为防御北方游牧部落侵袭而修筑的规模浩大的军事工程。早在春秋战国时期，各国诸侯为便修筑烽火台，并用城墙连接起来，形成了最早的长城。长城并不只是一道单独的城墙，而是由城墙、敌楼、关城、墩堡、营城、卫所、烽火台等多种防御工事组成的一个完整的防御工程体系。

秦始皇灭六国之后，将原来秦国、赵国和燕国北边原有的长城连接起来。修筑长城是一个浩大的工程，秦始皇先后征用了近百万劳工，劳工数量甚至占到秦朝全国总人口的二十分之一。修筑长城是一项艰苦的工作，长城修筑在崇山峻岭、峭壁深壑之上，当时没有任何机械化设备，全部劳动都由人力和简单的工具来完成。古代工匠在修筑长城的过程中，积累了丰富的经验：从确定长城的走向，到整个防御体系的配置，都"因地形，用险制塞"。长城大多建在山梁上，内侧为缓坡。在穿越河谷的地段，或以沟堑代替墙壁，或在河谷一侧增筑一段平行的墙壁。两山之间的长城则用天然石块砌成石墙，形成"石门"。还有城墙的结构形制、选材用料，都巧妙地就地取材、因材施用，其巧妙、合理的构思令人叹为观止。德国著名考古学家希里曼曾这样赞美长城："中国长城，我从孩童时代每次听到人说起就感觉到一股炽烈的好奇心，现在我亲眼看到了，它的伟大超过我想象中的一百倍。我越长久地注视这个壮伟的防御工程和它令人惊怖的多角的堡塞，不断地向最高的山脊背上攀缘着，它对于我越像是洪水以前巨人族的神话式的创造。"

有了长城的阻挡，军队可化被动为主动，亦可转守为攻，攻守自如。同时，长城对边远地区经济的发展也起到了积极的作用。长城沿线大多是生产比较落后的地区，人烟稀少，土地荒凉。而长城为了解决守城将士军备给养的供应问题，还需要加强边境地区的开发建设，甚至移民前往开发，进行农牧业生产。此外，长城在文化艺术上的价值，也足以与其在历史和战略上的重要性相媲美。两千多年来，以长

● 山海关长城

山海关位于河北省秦皇岛市东北部，始建于1381年，城墙全长约26千米，是明代长城的东北起点，也是万里长城的入海口。山海关以城为关，平面呈四方形，整个城关的面积约192平方千米。山海关是一座防御体系比较完整的关城，在其东、西、南、北四个方向共建有主城门四座，各城门上均修筑城楼。在东、西门外分别修筑有瓮城一座，城外有护城河等其他坚固的防御工事。

The Great Wall at Shanhai Pass

Shanhai Pass, constructed in 1381, is located in the northeast of Qinhuangdao City, Hebei Province and obtains a total length of 26 kilometres. It is the start point of the northeast part of the Great Wall where the wall meets the ocean. Shanhai Pass is a square city, occupying approximately 192 square kilometres. As a comparatively completed defensive system, there are four main gates on its four directions respectively, with one gate tower on each main gate. Outside the gates in the east and west there are the barbican and there is a moat with other fortifications around the barbican.

城为中心，南北各民族不断交流，促进了各民族文化的发展，也形成了一种有别于其他地区的文化地带。时至今日，长城虽然早已失去了其原本的军事价值，但它所承载的中国两千多年的历史却像一部百科全书，向世界讲述着中国古代的政治、经济、建筑等多方面的发展和成就，具有很高的科学价值、历史价值和文化价值。

● 陕北延安秦长城遗址（图片提供：全景正片）

延安境内的秦长城遗址全长约235千米，是战国时期秦昭襄王二十五年（前282年）为防御匈奴南下侵扰而修建的。

Relics of the Great Wall of the Qin Dynasty in Yan'an City, Northern Shaanxi Province

The Great Wall relics in Yan'an are totally 235 kilometres long. This part of the Great Wall was built in the 25th year (282 B.C.)of King Zhaoxiang of State Qin in the Warring States Period (475 B.C.-221 B.C.), served as a frontier of defense against Xiongnu's harassment.

秦以后，西汉、东汉、北魏、北齐、北周、隋、辽、金、明等各代，均大规模修筑或增筑长城。明代是长城修筑史上的最后一个朝代，其修筑规模之宏大、防御组织之完备、所用建筑材料之坚固，都大大超越了以往各个朝代，建筑体量巨大，气势磅礴。

The Construction of the Great Wall

The Great Wall is a vast military project to protect from the invasion and harassment of nomadic tribes in the north in different stages of Chinese history. Early in the Spring and Autumn Period and Warring States Period (770 B.C. – 221 B.C.), each state built up smoke towers and linked them with walls, regarded as the rudiment of the Great Wall. The Great wall is never a sole wall but the integrated fortifications consisted of walls, watchtowers, *Guancheng* (frontier pass city), citadels, barracks, garrisons and smoke towers.

  Qin Shihuang connected the Great Wall existing in States Qin, Zhao and northern Yan after defeating the other six states. The construction of the Great Wall was a huge undertaking and Qin Shihuang conscripted nearly one million labors to finish the project, occupying approximately one twentieth of the total population of the Qin Dynasty (221 B.C.-206 B.C.). The Great Wall was constructed on high mountains and lofty hills, across dangerous cliffs and deep valleys. Without any mechanized equipment, all works were completed by manpower and oversimplified tools, making this an extremely arduous task. The ancient craftsmen gathered rich experience in the construction process and followed the principle of "adjusting measures to local geographic conditions" in determining the route and designing the whole defense system. Generally, the Great Wall was built on mountains with the inner sides more gentle. It is common to employ two methods while building walls across the valleys: one is to use the ditch as the wall and the other one is to construct a wall paralleling to one side of the valley. The walls across two mountains are protected by natural stones as the outer layer, forming the "stone pass". The craftsmen applied local building materials to the construction and conducted the design according to the local geographic conditions ingeniously, demonstrating the delicacy and exquisiteness of this breathtaking engineering project. The famous German archeologist Heinrich Schilemann once praised the Great Wall: "Every time I heard people mentioned the Great Wall of China in my childhood, I was fired with the blazing curiosity. Now, I saw it myself, its mightiness and magnificence are much greater than my imagination. To me, the longer I witness this great fortification with its amazing watchtowers and citadels, as they are challenging the highest mountain in the world, the more similarities it shares with the Giants' creation before the Deluge."

  Thanks to the separation of the Great Wall, the troops could perform more active and change the situation from defense to attack, making it easy to transfer the statement of offensive and defensive. Meanwhile, the Great Wall played a positive role in the development process of the remote regions. Along the walls, most areas were suffered with relatively retarded production mode, with sparse population and desolate lands. It was necessary to strengthen the growth and construction of border regions. In order to support those guarding soldiers, people were even introduced from other places to these areas to develop the local agriculture and animal husbandry. What is more, the cultural and artistic values of the Great Wall can be compared with its values in history and strategy. For more than two thousand years, the Great Wall witnessed that people from different ethnic groups in both south and north communicated with each other continuously and this promotes the cultural development of each ethnic group, forming a unique cultural zone differing from other regions. Nowadays, although the Great Wall has lost its previous military values, it performs as an encyclopedia containing the more than two thousand years' Chinese history. The Great Wall is regarded as a symbol of the developments and achievements in political, economic and architectural areas, obtaining extremely high scientific, historic and cultural values.

  After the Qin Dynasty (221 B.C.-206 B.C.), emperors of many dynasties conducted large-scale construction of Great Wall, including dynasties of Western Han (206 B.C.-25 A.D.), Eastern Han (25-220), Northern Wei (386-534), Northern Qi (550-577), Northern Zhou (557-581), Sui (581-618), Liao (907-1125), Jin (1115-1234) and Ming (1368-1644). As the last Great Wall construction, the large scale, perfect defensive system and solid building materials of the Great Wall of the Ming Dynasty exceed that of all other dynasties significantly, with its magnificence and immensity in scale and appearance.

• 河北金山岭长城

金山岭长城位于河北省承德市滦平县境内，是明朝爱国将领戚继光主持修筑的，全长10.5千米，沿线设有关隘5处，敌楼67座，烽火台3座。金山岭长城是万里长城的精华地段，视野开阔，敌楼密集，建筑艺术精美，军事防御体系健全。

The Jinshanling Great Wall in Hebei Province

The Jinshanling Great Wall is located in Luanping County of Chengde City in Hebei Province, constructed by the famous patriotic military general Qi Jiguang in the Ming Dynasty (1368-1644). It is 10.5 kilometres long with 5 mountain passes, 67 watchtowers and 3 smoke towers. As the essence of the Great Wall, Jinshanling Great Wall obtains broad vision, intensive watchtowers, delicate architectures and perfect military fortifications.

秦始皇陵
The Mausoleum of Qin Shihuang

秦始皇陵是秦始皇嬴政的陵墓，简称"秦陵"，被誉为"世界第八大奇迹"。1987年，秦始皇陵与兵马俑被列入《世界遗产名录》。

据史料记载，嬴政从13岁即位时就开始修建自己的陵园，后由丞相李斯主持规划和设计，大将章邯负责监工，修筑时间前后长达39年。秦始皇陵墓工程之浩大、气魄之宏伟，开历代封建统治者奢侈厚葬之先例。

The tomb of the first emperor (Ying Zheng) of the Qin Dynasty (221 B.C.-206 B.C.), is also called the Mausoleum of Qin Shihuang and honored as the Eighth Wonder of the World. It was included on the World Heritage List in 1987 with Terracotta Warriors.

According to historical documents, Ying Zheng started to build his mausoleum the moment he ascended to throne at 13. Li Si, the prime minister, was put in charge of the overall planning and designing. The senior general, Zhang Han was appointed to supervise the project. The construction lasted for as long as 39 years. The mausoleum of Qin Shihuang, with its unprecedented size and magnificence, is considered as the start of the luxurious imperial mausoleums and funerals, which were later inherited in the following feudal dynasties in ancient China.

> 皇陵的选址

秦始皇陵位于陕西省西安市临潼区东5千米处，距西安市37千米。秦始皇陵南倚骊山，北临渭水，依山面水，极具气魄。

秦陵修建的位置与秦国前几代国君陵墓的位置有着密切的关系。秦始皇先祖的陵园位于临潼区以西的芷阳一带，而秦始皇陵园是选在芷阳以东的骊山脚下。这是因为中国古代帝王陵墓往往按照生前居住时的尊卑、上下排列，长者在西、晚辈居东。所以，秦始皇陵园选在骊山脚下是秦国的礼制决定的。

另外，陵墓位置的选择也与当时"依山造陵"的风水习俗相关。大约自春秋开始，各诸侯国国君相继兴起了"依山造陵"的丧葬风

> Site Selection of the Imperial Mausoleum

The Mausoleum of Qin Shihuang was located 5 kilometres east of Lintong County in Shaanxi Province and 37 kilometres from Xi'an City. The mausoleum with magnificent view, was shadowed by Lishan Mountain in the south, and overlooked Weishui River in the north.

The location of the Mausoleum of Qin Shihuang referred to the mausoleum sites of the former monarchs of State Qin. The ancestral cemetery of Qin Shihuang was located in Zhiyang, west of Lintong County. According to the ancient burial custom that the imperial mausoleums should be built in the order of seniority (the elder one in the west and the younger one in the east), the mausoleum of Qin Shihuang was located at the foot of Lishan Mountain, in the east of Zhiyang.

• 秦始皇陵
The Mausoleum of Qin Shihuang

气。许多国君墓不是背山面河，就是面对视野开阔的平原，甚至有的国君墓建在山巅之上，以显示生前的崇高地位和王权的威严肃穆。

春秋战国时期的秦国君主墓更是承袭了"依山造陵"的旧俗，因此秦始皇陵建造在骊山脚下也就不足为奇了。秦始皇陵依山面水，有着优美的自然环境和静谧肃穆的格局。整个骊山唯有临潼区东这一段山脉海拔较高，山势起伏不定，重峦叠嶂。从渭河北岸远眺，这段山脉左右对

Therefore, the site selection of the Mausoleum of Qin Shihuang was determined by the ritual system of State Qin.

In addition, its site selection also took into account the *Fengshui* tradition at that time, which believed that tombs should be built near mountains. Such tradition started to prevail among the monarchs of vassal states from the Spring and Autumn Period (770 B.C. - 476 B.C.). Some of them located their tombs on mountainsides, overlooking the river or the open plain. And several monarchs even built their tombs on the top of the mountain to demonstrate their lofty standing and solemnity of kingship.

Mausoleums of the monarchs of State Qin in the Spring and Autumn Period also followed this old tradition, thus it stands to reason that the Mausoleum of Qin Shihuang was positioned at the foot of Lishan Mountain. The mountain and river offer the site a graceful natural landscape with a solemn silence. Lishan Mountain gains higher altitude when it reaches the east of Lintong County with rolling hills and peaks rising one after another. When overlooking the landscape from the north

称，像是一个巨大的屏风立于秦始皇陵之后。如若站在秦始皇陵顶南望，这段山脉又呈弧形排列，皇陵位于骊山峰峦环抱之中，与整个骊山呈现出浑然一体的景象。

秦朝"依山环水"的陵墓选址观念对后世皇朝的建陵习俗产生了极为深远的影响。

bank of the Weishui River, one finds that the symmetrical stretch of mountain range serves as a large screen at the back of the Mausoleum of Qin Shihuang. If one stands at the top of the mausoleum and overlooks to the south, one finds that the mountain range curves around the mausoleum to fully embrace it, and the mausoleum fits into the scenery in a natural and harmonious way.

The tradition of site selection that people should build tombs near mountains and rivers was adopted in the Qin Dynasty (221 B.C.-206 B.C.), had a very profound influence on the customs of imperial mausoleum construction in the following dynasties.

骊山

骊山是秦岭山脉的一个支峰，东西绵延约20千米，最高海拔1302米，山形秀丽，峰峦起伏。骊山非常奇特，山上四季有长青之树，三春有飘香之花，景色迷人。骊山峰峦起伏，远远望去，好似一匹凝神远眺、跃跃欲奔的骏马——骊山也因此得名。

骊山早在3000多年前的西周时期，就是帝王将相们的游乐宝地。周、秦、汉、唐以来，这里一直是名胜，曾营建过许多离宫别院。

Lishan Mountain

Lishan Mountain is part of the Qinling Mountains, stretching 20 kilometres east to west and rising 1,302 metres above the sea level. People find that Lishan Mountain is of unique beauty: there are trees that never wither away and flowers that bloom throughout the spring and rolling mountain ranges that look like galloping horses.

More than 3,000 years ago, early in the Western Zhou Dynasty (1046 B.C.-771 B.C.), Lishan Mountain was employed by the emperors as a place for entertainment. Many imperial resorts were built in Lishan Mountain as the mountain has historically been a place of interest from the Zhou Dynasty (1046 B.C.-221 B.C.), the Qin Dynasty (221 B.C.-206 B.C.), the Han Dynasty (206 B.C.-220 A.D.) down to the Tang Dynasty (618-907).

• 骊山风光
Landscape of Lishan Mountain

> 皇陵的修建

皇帝或国君在活着的时候就修建陵墓，是古代各王朝的风俗。秦始皇陵的修建伴随着秦始皇嬴政的执政生涯，前后共修造了39年，一直到秦始皇去世时都没有竣工。秦二世胡亥继位后，又修建了一年多，皇陵才基本完工，其修建的时间比埃及胡夫金字塔还要长8年。

关于秦陵工程，《史记·秦始皇本纪》中曾记载秦始皇陵"穿三泉"（穿凿三重地下水），《汉旧书》中对秦始皇陵的描述也有"已深已极""深极不可入"之语。

自嬴政即位到统一全国的26年为陵园工程的初期。这一阶段先后展开了陵园工程的设计和主体工程的施工，初步奠定了陵园工程的规模和基本格局。

> Construction of the Imperial Mausoleum

In ancient China, emperors and monarchs started to build their burial place when they were alive. It is an old tradition followed in all dynasties. The construction of the mausoleum of Qin Shihuang proceeded for 39 years until his death. When Hu Hai, Emperor the Second of the Qin Dynasty (230 B.C.-207 B.C.), has been enthroned for more than one year, the construction of the mausoleum was just basically completed. It lasted 8 years longer than constructing the Khufu Pyramid in Egypt.

In *Biography of Qin Shihuang* from *Shiji* (*Shiji, Historical Records*, written by Sima Qian), it was documented that the project of Mausoleum of Qin Shihuang had dug through three layers of groundwater. In *Ancient Documents of the Han Dynasty*, the mausoleum was described as the deepest mausoleum

• 秦咸阳一号宫殿复原模型

一号宫殿台顶建楼两层，下层建围廊和敞厅，使全台外观如同三层，非常壮观。上层正中为主体建筑，周围及下层分别为卧室、过厅、浴室等。下层有回廊，廊下以砖铺地，檐下有卵石散水。

Restoration Model of the First Palace in Xianyang City of the Qin Dynasty(221 B.C.-206 B.C.)
A two-storey pavilion was built on the platform of the first palace. Colonnades and open halls were built on the lowest floor, making its whole structure a spectacular three-storey look. On the upper floor the main building sat in the middle, while bedrooms, vestibules and bathrooms were built next to the main building or on the lowest floor. Winding corridors were also arranged on the lowest floor, tiled with bricks. Pebbles were paved on the ground under eaves to let water drain away.

从统一全国到秦始皇三十五年（前212年），前后历时9年的时间，为陵园工程的大规模修建时期。据记载，最多时有72万名囚徒或匠人来此大规模地进行工程修建。这段时期基本完成了陵园的主体工程。

ever, impossible for one to reach.

The first twenty-six years from Ying Zheng ascending the throne until he unified China was the first stage of the mausoleum project. Over the first stage, the designing has been finished and work on the main project has been started, laying down the scale and basic layout of the project.

- **一号坑的门道**

  俑坑四边各有5条门道，是当时施工的斜坡道。完工后，门道口即用立木封堵。

  Doorways in the Pit No.1

  On each side of one pit there are five doorways, which were used as ramps when the work was carried out. After the work was finished, the entrance would be blocked with standing wood timbers.

自秦始皇三十五年到秦二世二年（前208年）冬，历时3年多时间，是工程的收尾阶段。这一阶段主要从事陵园的收尾工程与覆土填埋任务。

尽管秦始皇陵工程历时如此之久，整个工程仍然没有按照预期理想完工。陵墓的修建被当

The next nine years until 212 B.C. was the second stage to carry out the project on a large scale. It was documented that there was a maximum of 720,000 prisoners and craftsmen gathering and working for the project at the same time. The main project was almost finished during this stage.

The last three years until the second winter after the Second Emperor of the Qin Dynasty took his power (the winter of 208 B.C.) was the final stage of the project. Over these three years, the remaining part of the project has been accomplished and then buried.

Although the construction has been

时爆发的波澜壮阔的陈胜、吴广农民大起义隔断。陈胜、吴广的下属周文将军率兵打到了陵园附近的戏水（今临潼区新丰镇附近）。面临大军压境、秦都咸阳被围之势，修筑秦陵的奴隶和囚徒们被武装起来，抵抗起义军。秦始皇陵园工程被迫结束。

lasting so long, the whole project still failed to finish on time. The construction was interrupted when a great peasant uprising led by Chen Sheng and Wu Guang happened. General Zhou Wen, leading a branch of the rebel army, attacked Xishui which was close to the mausoleum (near today's Xinfeng Town in Lintong District). At that time, Xianyang, Qin's capital city, was severely threatened because it had already been besieged by the army troops. Thus working slaves and prisoners were armed and sent to wars against the revolt and the project was forced to stop.

天怒人怨的皇陵

秦始皇陵的修建曾经让无数人家破人亡、妻离子散。修筑如此庞大的陵墓工程，使用的匠人和囚徒不计其数。最多的一次征发了70多万名工人，这是古今中外历史上修建一座帝王陵墓用人最多的一次。

与此同时，修建陵墓所需的石料数量也是骇人听闻的。这些石料需要成千上万的人从渭河北面的山上运送到打石场。在打石场，这些不规则的石头还需要打磨成所需要的形状。

Imperial Mausoleum Fueled People's Discontent and Anger

Construction of the Mausoleum of Qin Shihuang ruined the wellbeing of countless families. To finish the project, innumerable prisoners and craftsmen were employed in the construction.

A maximum of over 700,000 workers were employed to work on the project at one time. The number of employed labors was a record high in the world history of constructing a single imperial mausoleum project.

Moreover, the number of building stones used in the project is shocking as well. Those stones were transferred by thousands of labors from northern Lishan Mountain to stone-processing sites, where irregular stones were processed and polished into needed shapes.

• 开采石头建造陵墓的工人模型（图片提供：FOTOE）
Model of Labors Quarrying Stones to Build the Mausoleum

> 皇陵的布局

秦始皇陵按照秦始皇驾崩后可以照样享受荣华富贵的理念，仿照秦国都城咸阳的布局建造而成，大体呈"回"字形结构，陵墓周围筑有内外两重城垣。由于秦始皇陵墓还未被发掘，根据目前探明的一些大型建筑，可以划分为寝殿、便殿、园寺吏舍等区域。陵园总面积为56.25平方千米，相当于78个北京故宫。

外城和内城

秦始皇陵墓的外城，即内城垣和外城垣的中间区域，是外廓城部分。

外城西区是地面和地下设施最为密集的区域，其中建筑基址约占据了西区空间的三分之二。外城的

> Layout of the Imperial Mausoleum

The Mausoleum of Qin Shihuang was constructed following the idea to allow him to keep all the glory in the world after his death. Its layout referred to that of Xianyang City, the capital city of State Qin. With a structure resembling the Chinese character *Hui* (回), the mausoleum was enclosed by inner and outer city walls. Since it has not been unearthed, based on some studied major buildings the mausoleum can be divided into areas such as bedding hall, side hall, mourners' chamber, etc. The total coverage of the cemetery is 56.25 square metres, 78 times as large as Forbidden City in Beijing.

Inner City and Outer City

The outer city of the Mausoleum of Qin

便殿遗址
Site of Side Palace

园寺吏舍遗址
Site of Mourners' Chambers

饮官遗址
Site of Feed-making Workshop

铜车马坑
Bronze Chariots and Horses Pit

曲尺形马厩坑
L-shaped Horse Stable Pit

地宫封土
Seal Mound of Underground Palace

内城
Inner City

陪葬坑
Pit

外城
Outer City

排水渠
Drainage Ditch

- **秦始皇陵布局图**

  秦始皇陵整体呈矩形设置，坐西向东，以封土区域为中心可以分为四层：第一层是外城以外的区域，第二层是外城，第三层是内城，第四层是地下宫城（地宫）。这是皇陵的核心区域。

  Layout of the Mausoleum of Qin Shihuang

  The Mausoleum of Qin Shihuang adopts a rectangular layout. It sits in the west to face the east. With the seal mound as its centre area, it can be divided into four layers from the outside in. The first layer is the area outside the outer city, the second layer is the outer city, the third layer is the inner city, and the forth layer is the underground palace, which is the core area of the imperial mausoleum.

秦始皇陵的设计思想

秦始皇陵的设计理念据研究大致有三方面内容。

一、事死如事生。中国古代始终有一种宗教观念，即认为人死后灵魂不灭，只是从人间转到了阴间继续生活。所以人生前所需和拥有的一切，死后也要有。

二、陵墓仿都城。在阶级社会里，陵墓的位置、大小和布局是权力和身份的象征。而一国之君的陵墓则要仿制都城的布局建制。

三、无上的皇权。秦始皇统一中国后，自认为功德至高，无人能及。这种思想不仅反映在他生前的行为上，还反映在陵园建设的思想中，即要达到前无古人、后无来者的效果。

Designing Concept of the Mausoleum of Qin Shihuang

According to studies, the designing concept of the Mausoleum of Qin Shihuang includes three major parts.

Firstly, the deceased deserves to be served the same as the alive. In ancient China, people believed that one's soul still existed and lived in the underworld after one died. Therefore what one owned when alive should be owned as well when one died.

Secondly, the imperial mausoleum should be built referring to the capital city. In a class society, the location, scale and layout of a mausoleum symbolize the power and status of the deceased. Thus, the emperor's mausoleum should be constructed based on the layout and organizational system of the capital city.

Thirdly, the imperial power should be supreme. After Qin Shihuang unified China, he considered his merits and virtues so great that no one could compete with him. This belief was not only reflected in his decisions when alive, but also was reflected in the construction of his burial place, that is, to be unprecedentedly magnificent, like no one else's of all time.

西区象征着秦都咸阳城的厩苑、囿苑及园寺吏舍，是供始皇帝玩乐游弋的地方。

秦始皇陵最外围区域是外城垣之外的地区，此处多为建设、陪葬

Shihuang, the area between the inner city wall and outer city wall, is the exterior part of the city.

The western part of the outer city has the highest concentrations of ground and underground facilities, among which

和管护秦始皇陵园而设置，属于秦始皇陵园的边围。在秦陵外围的东边，除分布着秦兵马俑坑外，还有98座小型马厩坑及众多陪葬墓。此处还有3处修陵人员的墓地和砖瓦烧制窑址。在北边还发现了藏有禽兽肢体及鳖的仓储坑、陵园督造人员的官署和郦邑建筑遗址。

foundation sites take up two thirds of the space. This part of outer city resemble the places for the entertainment of Qin Shihuang.

The outermost area of the Mausoleum of Qin Shihuang is outside the outer city walls. The facilities are mostly arranged here, on the edge of the cemetery, for constructing mausoleum,

- **K9901陪葬坑挖掘现场**

K9901陪葬坑位于秦始皇陵封土东南的内外城垣之间，为地下坑道式土木结构，平面略呈"凸"字形，总面积约800平方米，内设3条过洞。这里出土了青铜大鼎1件、陶俑11件及兵器、车马器等遗物。

Excavation Site of K9901 Pit of Funeral Objects

The K9901 pit is located between the inner and outer city walls at the southeast of the underground palace. Its underground galleries adopted the tunnel-type structure, presenting a bulging plane structure as Chinese character "凸". Its total coverage reaches 800 square metres and it has three walkways. A large bronze cauldron, eleven pottery figurines, along with some other relics including weapons and chariots and horse fittings have been unearthed from this pit.

• 秦陵中出土的陶器盖
Pottery Cover Unearthed from the Mausoleum of Qin Shihuang

　　在秦始皇陵园南部和骊山相接的地方，有一条宽约40米的防洪堤，用以阻挡来自骊山的洪水，保护秦始皇陵墓，使其免遭水患。

　　秦陵外城的西北角以外有一个大型的石料加工厂，面积约75万平方米。在这里，考古人员发现了许多建筑材料、生产工具和生活用具，如瓦当、铁锤、铁铲、陶盆、石磨等。

　　内城分布着许多建筑，例如用于祭祀和用于陪葬的建筑群落。作为当时秦始皇陵的重点建设区，此

keeping funeral objects and maintaining cemetery. In addition to the terracotta warriors pits, there are 98 small stables pits and subordinate tombs in the east. Three historic sites of workers' tombs and brick kilns were also unearthed here. In the north, people discovered storage pit with bodies of animals and soft-shelled turtles, and historic sites of project supervisors' offices and Liyi folk buildings.

　　On the south of the Mausoleum of Qin Shihuang where it borders Lishan Mountain, a 40 metres wide levee was

- **K0006陪葬坑挖掘现场**

此坑位于秦始皇陵封土西南约50米处，是一座地下坑道式土木结构建筑，平面呈东西向的"中"字形，由斜坡门道、前室和后室组成，总面积约410平方米。该坑出土了陶俑12件、铜钺4件、木车一辆和葬马20余件。出土器物上"中厩"、"宫厩"、"左厩"、"大厩"、"小厩"等文字，显示这一区域应该是宫廷厩苑或军马场。

Excavation Site of K0006 Pit

This pit is located 50 metres east of the seal mound. Adopting a wood-and-earth structure, its underground galleries consists of a slope doorway stretching from east to west, a front room and a back room, together assembling the Chinese character Zhong (中). It is overall 410 square metres and from this pit 12 earthen figurines, 4 bronze battle axes, 1 wood chariot, and more than 20 horse skeletons have been unearthed. Some of those pieces bear characters including "Mid-size Stable", "Palace Stable", "Left Stable", "Large-size Stable" and "Small-size Stable". It shows that this area was used as the royal stable garden or army horse-keeping farm.

处设施相对较多，尤其是内城的南半部分更为密集。秦始皇陵的寝殿、车马仪仗队伍、仓储室等均设置在南半部。内城北半部的西区是便殿的附属建筑区，东区则是后宫人员的陪葬墓区。

built so that the site wouldn't be drowned by floods coming from Lishan Mountain.

Outside the northeast corner of the outer city, there is a large stone-processing site with a coverage of 750,000 square metres. The archaeologists found many building materials, instruments of production and daily tools, including eave tiles, iron hammers, shovels, earthenware pots, stone mills, etc.

There are many buildings in the inner city, for example, the building groups where people offered sacrifices and buildings used as funeral objects. As the main construction project, more

封土的西北方建有饮官官署。饮官即古时掌管墓主人饮食的官员，饮官官署相当于明清皇宫里的御膳房。现饮官官署遗址2000多平方米，地面上存有用木头砌成的墙，上面铺有木板，考古人员还在这里挖掘出了大量的陶瓮、陶盆和陶罐。

在秦陵的东面、距离封土约4千米的地方存有一个秦阙。"阙"即古代在宫、庙或墓门外所建的两

• 秦陵中出土的陶壶
Pottery Pot Unearthed from the Mausoleum of Qin Shihuang

facilities were arranged there, especially the southern inner city where the bedding palace, guards of honor with chariots and horses, and storage rooms were built. In northern inner city, there were auxiliary buildings of the side palace on the west and subordinate tombs of concubines on the east.

To the northwest of the seal mound was an office for officials who provided food and drink to the host of the mausoleum. This office was used like the imperial kitchen in the Ming Dynasty (1368-1644) and the Qing Dynasty (1616-1911). The historic site of this office is over 2,000 square metres. There are wood walls covered with wood planks above the ground and a great number of pottery jars, basins and pots have been unearthed.

In the east of the mausoleum, 4 kilometres from the seal mound, stands a *Que* (watchtower on either side of a palace gate). In ancient China, people built two lofty platforms called *Que* outside the gate of palace, temple or mausoleum. The *Que* of the Mausoleum of Qin Shihuang has been destroyed but its remaining part over 2 metres high is still a good display of the flourishing period in the past. One enters

- 陪葬坑中的立柱

立柱的直径为30厘米，间距1.1—1.5米，上端承托着梁枋。

Columns in the Pit

With the diameter of 30 centimetres, the columns were spaced at various intervals between 1.1 metres to 1.5 metres to support the beam.

- 陪葬坑的地面砖

坑内地面是夯筑的，夯土厚约45厘米。夯土上用秦砖铺地，不错缝，排列整齐。

Floor Tiles in the Pit

The rammed earth floor of the pit is 45 centimetres thick, neatly tiled with Qin bricks without staggered joints.

• 秦陵中出土的陶盆
Earthenware Pots Unearthed from the Mausoleum of Qin Shihuang

个高大的台子。这个秦阙虽已残缺不全，但仍有两米多高，彰显着昔日的繁华景象。进入秦阙，也就走进了秦陵的墓道，可见秦陵的正门是向东的。

地宫

秦始皇陵墓布局的核心是地宫，其他如城垣、建筑、陪葬墓、陪葬坑等皆围绕着地宫修建。对于地宫，迄今为止依然谜团重重，因

the mausoleum pathway through *Que*, therefore people tell the main gate of the mausoleum is facing the east.

Underground Palace

The core of the layout of the Mausoleum of Qin Shihuang is the underground palace. The rest including city walls, buildings were all arranged surrounding the core palace. Nevertheless, the underground palace is still a puzzle to the world, as there is no detailed description

● 秦陵地宫微缩模型（图片提供：FOTOE）
Miniature Model of the Underground Palace

为史书典籍没有翔实的记载。而依靠现在的科技手段，也无法探测清楚地宫内部的形制和结构。目前只能根据历史典籍的只言片语来猜测和利用现有的科技手段加以窥探。

秦陵地宫相当于秦咸阳都城的宫城。地宫位于内城南半部的巨大的封土堆下面，封土是用一层层黄土坚实地夯筑而成，经过两千多年，夯土依然细腻结实，完好如初。在封土堆下墓室的周围存在着一圈很厚的细夯土墙，这就是地宫

in any historical documents or accounts. Moreover, it is not possible to detect its internal pattern and structure with existing modern technology. At present, people can only peek at the underground palace based on a few documented descriptions and available technology.

The actual location of the underground palace reflects that of the imperial palace of Xianyang City, the capital city of State Qin. It is buried in the southern inner city under a huge mound of earth. The huge mound was

的宫墙。秦始皇的墓室位于地宫的中央区域，高约15米，相当于一个标准的足球场大小。

为了保持地宫排水顺畅，防止地宫被水淹没，修筑地宫的工匠在秦陵周围修建了规模巨大的防水墙。防水墙长约1千米，底部由厚达17米的防水性强的清膏泥夯筑而成，上部由84米宽的黄土夯成。这种设计非常科学和巧妙——秦始皇陵园的地势东南高、西北低，落差达85米，而这样的排水结构正好挡

constructed with layers of loess, rammed firmly. After 2,000 years, the layers are still fine and solid, and remains intact. The burial chamber is surrounded by thick rammed earthen walls, namely the palace walls of the underground palace. Qin Shihuang's burial chamber was located in the middle of the underground palace. With a height of 15 metres, it is equal to the size of a standard soccer field.

To make sure the drainage unhindered and to prevent water logging, the craftsmen who built the underground

- 秦陵出土的瓦棺
Earthen Coffin Unearthed from the Mausoleum of Qin Shihuang

住了地下水由高向低处渗透，有效地保护了地宫。

《史记》描述秦陵地宫"上具天文，下具地理"。据考古学家推断，《史记》中"上具天文"应当是指秦陵墓室顶部的日、月、星象图，而"下具地理"则是指地宫中有代表着山川河湖的水银。有人推断，秦陵地宫上部可能绘有更为完整的二十八星宿图。

《史记》中还记载秦始皇陵

palace have constructed a huge water resistant wall around the Mausoleum of Qin Shihuang, about 1,000 metres long. The bottom of the wall was a 17 metres thick layer of rammed green past mud, which is a kind of strong waterproof material. The top of the wall was made of rammed loess, 84 metres wide. It was smartly designed with reason. The Mausoleum of Qin Shihuang is higher in the southeast and lower in the northwest with a drop of 85 metres. Thus the

- 云南大理玉皇阁大殿顶层的藻井绘画《二十八星宿图》（图片提供：FOTOE）
Chart of Twenty-eight Lunar Mansions Painting on the Top Floor's Roof of the Hall of Yuhuang Tower in Dali, Yunnan Province

• 五角形下水管道
Pentagon Sewer Line

"奇器珍怪徙藏满之"，藏品有"金雁""珠玉""翡翠"等。但是，地宫中到底珍藏了哪些奇珍异宝，在打开之前仍是一个谜团。

对秦始皇陵地宫的挖掘，目前的技术水平还达不到，开启的时机还不成熟。如果贸然挖掘地宫，存在几千年之久的地宫环境将被破坏，这会给地下文物造成不可逆转的毁灭性破坏。

drainage system has well prevented the ground water permeating to the lower place to keep the underground palace dry and safe.

According to *Shiji* (*Historical Records*), the underground palace of Mausoleum of Qin Shihuang has everything from the sky to the land. It is inferred by the experts that the elements from the sky should refer to the sun, the moon and the star chart painted or carved on the chamber's roof, while the elements

陵墓里的长明灯

在中国古代，侯王贵族乃至一般平民的墓穴里都会设置长明灯，即在棺椁四周放置瓷灯台或一盏盏铜灯台。据《史记》记载，秦陵地宫中有以鱼油制成的长明灯。这些长明灯永久不熄，使地宫如同白昼。长明灯不仅具有装饰作用，更是帝王一生荣耀的彰显。

Eternal Lamp in Tombs

In ancient China, both noble and common people would have eternal lamp in their tombs. They placed porcelain or bronze lamp stands around the coffin. According to *Shiji*, the eternal lamp in the underground palace of the Mausoleum of Qin Shihuang consumes fish oil, dispelling the underground darkness and bringing the eternal light to the palace. The eternal lamp is not only a decoration, but is more about showing off the emperor's lifetime glory.

of the land should refer to the mercury that represents rivers and lakes in the underground palace. Someone thinks that there is a complete chart of the 28 lunar mansions painted on the roof of the underground palace.

According to *Shiji*, the Mausoleum of Qin Shihuang is full of rare and precious antiques, including gold geese, jewelries, jades, etc. However, the treasures stored in the underground palace will still remain a puzzle until the palace is open.

It is still not a good time to excavate the underground palace as the present technology is not prepared. Opening the palace without careful consideration will destroy the thousand-year underground environment, which will at last result in irreversible and devastating damages to the underground antiques.

中国古代的墓室构造

中国古代陵墓的建筑构造有一个发展过程。东汉以前的墓室为竖穴式,即从地面向地下挖一个大方坑,棺椁放置在方坑的中央,四周放置陪葬品,然后埋上土。春秋以前的墓上没有封土堆,与地面平齐,称为"墓"。据史料记载,伟大的思想

- **清西陵崇陵地宫**

清西陵位于河北易县的永宁山下,是清初营建的一处规模较大的陵墓区。崇陵是光绪皇帝(1871—1908)死后才开始修建的,也是中国最后一座帝王陵墓。崇陵地宫虽规制并不宏大,但工料之精、耗银之多也是相当可观的。墓道有四重石门,每重门由两扇整雕的青白玉石合成,上面有菩萨浮雕一尊。地宫内床为青石雕成的须弥座,上面并排停放着光绪皇帝和其皇后的棺椁。

Underground Palace of the Chongling Mausoleum, Western Qing Tombs (Qing Dynasty, 1616-1911)

The Western Qing Tombs, located at the foot of Yongning Mountain of Yixian County in Hebei Province, were a large mausoleum area built in the early Qing Dynasty. The Chongling Mausoleum, started after Emperor Guangxu's (1871-1908) death, was the last imperial mausoleum in China. Its underground palace is not very big in scale, but it is of considerable fine materials with great costs. There are four stone doors standing in the path leading to the underground palace. Each door, with a relief of Bodhisattva, is combined by two pieces of green and white marble stones, each separately carved out of an entire piece of stone. The bed in the underground palace was made out of bluestone and shaped like a sumeru. On the bed there are the Emperor Guangxu and his wife's coffins next to each other.

● 汉茂陵

茂陵是西汉武帝刘彻（前156—前87）的陵墓，位于陕西兴平市东北。茂陵陵园呈方形，分为内、外两城，四周环以围墙，边长约430米。茂陵的封土为上小下大的覆斗形，现存残高46.5米，冢底边长约240米。汉武帝的梓宫（棺木）共有五棺二椁，外层是"黄肠题凑"。"黄肠题凑"是流行于西汉时期的一种特殊葬制，使用者主要是帝王及其妻妾，还有皇帝特许的宠臣。"黄肠"是指墓葬的材料——去皮的柏木黄心，"题凑"是指墓葬的形式，木与椁壁板呈垂直方向垒砌于椁室四周，木头皆内向。汉武帝梓宫的黄肠题凑由长90厘米、高宽各10厘米的15880根柏木堆叠而成。

Maoling Mausoleum (Western Han Dynasty, 206 B.C. -25 A.D.)

The Maoling Mausoleum, the tomb of Liu Che, the Emperor Wu of the Western Han Dynasty, was located in Maoling Village, the northeast of the Xingping City in Shaanxi Province. Its cemetery adopted a square layout and was divided into the inner city and the outer city, surrounded by city walls. The length of one side of its city walls is about 430 metres. The seal mound of Maoling Mausoleum, with small top and big bottom, assembles an inverted funnel shape. The relic of the mausoleum is 46.5 metres high and the side length of the bottom is about 240 metres. The emperor's catalpa coffin consists of five inner coffins and two outer coffins, with *Huangchang Ticou* (Yellow Cypress Wall) outside the outer coffin. *Huangchang Ticou* was a funeral system prevailed in the Western Han Dynasty. The main users were emperors, emperor's wives and concubines, and a few ministers with the emperor's special permission. *Huangchang* referred to peeled cypress wood with yellow core (*Huang* for yellow, *Chang* for gut), which was the material used to make the outer coffin. *Ticou* refers to the wall pattern. It means that these timbers, pointing to the inside, were placed vertical to the wall boards of the outer coffin and therefore built into a wall. The *Huangchang Ticou* of outside the outer coffin in the Maoling Mausoleum was built with 15,880 yellow cypress timbers. Each of them is processed 90 centimetres long, 10 centimetres wide and 10 centimetres high.

家孔子常周游列国，他担心回家后找不到父母的墓，便在墓上堆了三尺高的土作为记号。从此，后人按照孔子的做法，也在墓上堆土。渐渐地，有钱有势的人墓上堆的土越来越高，称为"陵"，而普通百姓的则称为"坟"。东汉以后，人们开始用砖或石在地上夯起墓室，建墓道进入。

秦陵墓室也为竖穴式，据《史记》记载，秦陵地宫挖得极深，直到地下水层，用铜液浇灌，并涂以丹漆，再在上面放棺椁。

Structure of the Coffin Chamber in Ancient China

The construction structure of coffin chambers in ancient China has undergone a development process. Coffin chambers before the Eastern Han Dynasty (25-220) adopted the vertical grave pattern, namely that one digs a square pit, places the coffin down in the middle of the pit surrounded by funeral objects and then buries the coffin. There was no grave mound before the Spring and Autumn Period (770 B.C. - 476 B.C.). The coffin chamber was buried underground with its top at ground level and called grave. According to historical documents, the great Chinese thinker Confucius was also a traveler. In case that he could not find his parents' graves, he piled up a mound of earth which was three *Chi* (*Chi*, an ancient Chinese unit for measuring distance. 1 *Chi* approximately equals to 23.1 centimetres at that time) high at the top of the graves. From then on, people began to pile up earth on graves to follow Confucius. Gradually, rich people piled huger and huger mounds on graves and their graves were called mausoleums. Common people's graves were called tombs. From the Eastern Han Dynasty, people built coffin chambers on the ground with rammed earth and stones, and paths leading to the coffin chambers.

The coffin chamber of Mausoleum of Qin Shihuang also adopted the vertical grave pattern. According to *Shiji*, the underground palace, extremely deep under the ground at the ground water level, was cast in bronze and painted with red paint. Coffins were kept down in the palace.

> 皇陵的防盗体系

根据正史和民间野史的记载，秦始皇陵的墓室里面堆满了随葬的奇珍异宝。为了防止被盗，秦陵的设计和修建者在里面设置了重重的机关和暗道。

根据《史记》中的记载："令匠作机弩矢，有所穿近者辄射之。"即秦陵针对盗墓贼的一个最为有效的措施就是在地宫中装设触发的机弩、箭矢。据后人推测，秦陵的机弩一般安放在墓门的后面，或是通往地宫的各个必经之处。有些机弩的箭头上可能还会涂抹毒性很强的毒汁，盗墓者一旦中箭，就会死亡。

后来的考古发现也证实了这一推测。秦始皇兵马俑坑曾出土过一种射程较远的大张力的劲弩。这种

> Security System of the Imperial Mausoleum

According to both official and unofficial historical accounts, there are a great number of extremely rare treasures stored in the burial chamber of the Mausoleum of Qin Shihuang. To safeguard the treasures, the mausoleum designers and builders developed an anti-theft system and equipped this place with many traps and secret channels.

It was documented in *Shiji* that the Qin court asked the craftsmen to set up crossbows so that anyone who approaches the tomb would be shot. The most effective anti-theft method adopted by the Mausoleum of Qin Shihuang is its crossbows with arrows and trigger mechanisms placed in the underground palace. People infer that the crossbows are most possibly placed behind doors or in any necessary place. Some arrow

弩弓靠人的臂力是根本不可能拉开的，但如果把这种弩弓一个个连接起来，通过机械发动使之丛射或是连发，就可达到无人操作、自行触发的目的。为了防止盗墓，在秦始皇陵墓门内、通道口等处安置上这种敏感的触发性武器。一旦不明真相的盗墓者进入墓穴，就会被这些放置在暗处的暗箭射杀。根据汉唐陵墓考古发现，秦代以后的皇帝陵墓中也普遍采用了类似的暗器。

heads were dipped in venom. If their targets were hit, they would have no chance to survive.

The later archaeological findings also proved this possibility. A kind of long-range crossbow has been unearthed from the terracotta army pit. This kind of crossbow is in no way operated by mankind, as it requires much greater strength. However, if these crossbows are arranged one by one and mechanically activated to shoot in bursts or

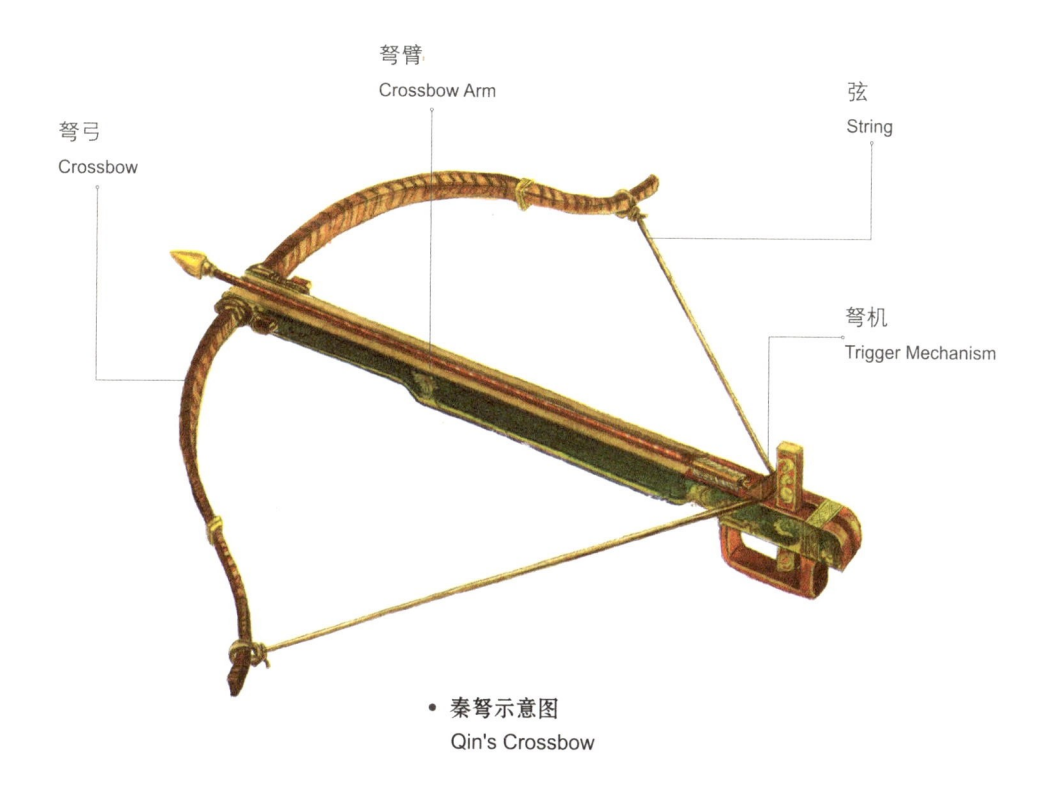

- 秦弩示意图
  Qin's Crossbow

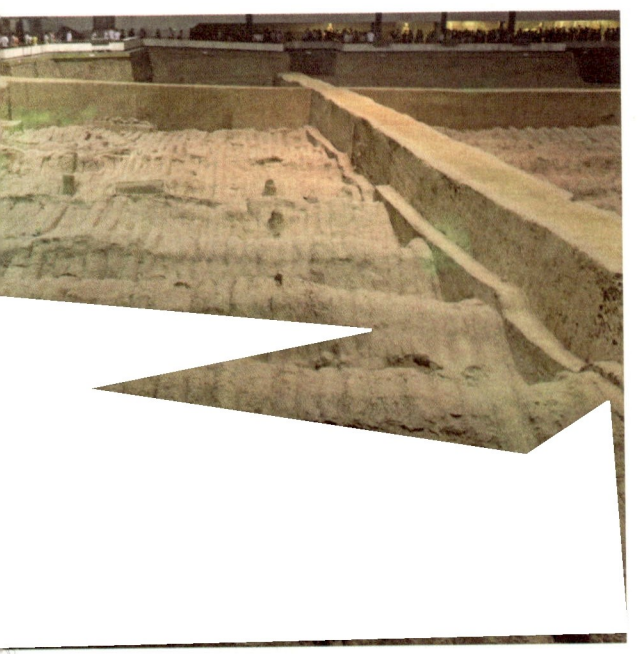

continuously, the purpose of unmanned operation and automatic triggering can be achieved. In order to prevent tomb robbery, this sensitive trigger weapon will be placed inside the tomb door and at the entrance of the passage. Once grave robbers entered the tomb without noticing the situation, they would be killed by arrows fired from nowhere. According to archeological findings on mausoleums in the Han Dynasty (206 B.C.-220 A.D.) and the Tang Dynasty (618-907), imperial mausoleums after the Qin Dynasty (221 B.C.-206 B.C.) generally employed similar hidden weapons with trigger mechanisms.

Additionally, it was documented in *Shiji* that there were mercury representing rivers and seas in the Mausoleum of Qin Shihuang. The underground palace was once injected with mercury to simulate the appearance of rivers, lackes and seas within the Qin Dynasty's territory. Mercury is a silvery liquid metal, very poisonous and volatile. Gaseous mercury will keep the body and funeral objects from rotting for hundreds of years. Moreover, mercury also prevents robbery. Grave robbers will be killed if they breathe in a certain amount of gaseous mercury.

- 隔梁

隔梁是夯筑的承重墙，宽约2.5米。上面的凹槽是棚木的印痕，黑色炭迹是棚木被烧后的遗存。

Partition Wall

The partition wall is the rammed bearing wall, about 2.5 metres wide. The notches were left by timbers. After the timbers caught fire, they left black trace.

另外，《史记》中还曾记载"（秦陵）以水银为百川江河大海"。秦陵地宫曾经模拟秦朝版图内江河湖海的样子注入水银（汞）。水银是一种含有剧毒的银白色状液体金属，具有较高的挥发性能，其蒸发出来的气体能使入葬的尸体和随葬品保持千年不腐。同时，水银还具有防盗的效果，如果盗墓贼在盗墓过程中吸入一定量的水银蒸气，就会死亡。

现代的考古科学探测表明，在秦陵封土中心1.2万平方米的范围内确实有一个强汞异常区，这些地区土壤中的汞含量高出周围地区4—8倍，这也许就是秦陵地宫中大量存

According to the modern scientific detection, within the coverage of 12,000 square metres at the center of the seal mound, there is an area with high mercury content. The mercury content in the soil is four to eight times more than that in other areas, which could possibly be the result left behind by the mercury starting to volatilize long time ago. People infer that, theoretically the amount of mercury

- **战车遗迹**
  考古学家在秦陵周围的陪葬坑中，发现了许多焚烧破坏的痕迹，但秦陵封土堆下的地宫却依然完好无损。

  Remains of War Chariot
  Archaeologists have found many traces of fire damage or other damages in the pits around the mausoleum. However, the underground palace stays unbroken.

- 秦代兵工厂

秦代兵器的制造已经引入标准化生产，不同产地的零部件可以组装在一起。

Military Factory (Qin Dynasty, 221 B.C.-206 B.C.)

Weapon production in the Qin Dynasty has introduced standard manufacturing. Components and parts of weapons were produced in different places and then assembled.

067

秦始皇陵

The Mausoleum of Qin Shihuang

在的水银长期挥发造成的结果。根据现今人们的推算，秦陵内原来藏有水银的理论数字应该为16255.2吨。封土里的水银分布是有规律的，东南、西南强，东北、西北较弱。如果以水银的分布来代表江海的话，这正好与中国河流由西往东汇入渤海、黄海的江河湖海的分布相符合。

当时，四川东南一带是汞的主要产地。从四川运输汞直至陕西秦陵，需要跨越长江、嘉陵江、汉水等数条大河，更需要翻越崇山峻岭。可以想见当时劳工付出的艰辛。

stored in the Mausoleum of Qin Shihuang should be 16,255.2 tons. The distribution of mercury in the seal mound is regular, weakening from southeast and southwest to northeast and northwest. If we see the distribution of mercury as China's rivers and seas, it does accord with China's river map, as China's rivers flow from east to west into the Bohai Sea and the Yellow Sea.

At that time, mercury was mainly produced in southeast Sichuan. The transport of mercury from Sichuan to the Mausoleum of Qin Shihuang in Shaanxi Province had to cross several major rivers including the Yangtze River, Jialing River and Hanshui River as well as towering and steep mountains. One can imagine how labors went through unimaginable hardship when building this project.

秦陵兵马俑
Terracotta Warriors in the Mausoleum of Qin Shihuang

秦始皇陵实质上是按照古代礼制"事死如事生"的要求特意设计的。"事死如事生",意思是死后也要和生前一样。中国古代的帝王崇信自己死后在阴间仍然过着类似阳间的生活,因而陵墓的地上、地下建筑和随葬生活用品均应仿照世间。

秦始皇即位后,大部分的精力和时间都投入统一全国的战争中。为了彰显自己生前史无前例的丰功伟绩,秦始皇选择以兵马俑作为自己的陪葬品。

兵马俑坑是位于秦始皇陵东侧1500米处的陪葬坑。这些兵马俑经历了2000多年的黄土掩埋。虽然现在有些陶俑变得支离破碎、残缺不全,但经过修复之后,展现在世人面前的庞大的兵俑阵仗和威严的将士面貌,仍然令人震撼。

Based on the specific requirement of Qin Shihuang, his mausoleum was designed on the basis of ancient ritual system of "honoring the dead as the living". The concept "honoring the dead as the living" means that the situation after death should be the same during his lifetime. Ancient imperial emperors in China pursued that after death, they would conduct a life in the nether world similar to that in the mortal world. Therefore, the constructions above and under the ground as well as the funeral objects should be manufactured as the real ones in this world.

After the enthronement, Qin Shihuang spent the majority of his energy and time in the unification wars. In order to manifest the unprecedented great achievements across his lifetime, he chose the Terracotta Warriors as his burial objects.

The Terracotta Warriors pits are located 1,500 metres east to the Mausoleum of Qin Shihuang. After more than 2,000 years' burial, some of the figurines are fragmented and incomplete in pieces. However, the magnificent pottery figurines of the enormous troops and majestic warriors presented to the world can still bring breathtaking and amazing experience to people.

> 偶然面世的奇迹

1974年3月11日，陕西省临潼县的一个农民在秦始皇陵园东侧1000米处的一片荒瘠的砂石地上挖井。在打井的过程中，这位农民发现了许多陶俑残片、铜镞和弩机等物品。其实，历史上这里的祖祖辈辈都有发现陶俑的经历，当地村民称这些陶俑为"瓦爷"。当地的村民将这次的发现向当地政府报告。临潼县文化局随即派人前往打井现场了解相关情况，并将挖井现场做了保护处理。县文化局的工作人员将挖掘到的文物带回了县里，经过几十天的努力，终于拼凑、修复起了几尊完整的武士俑。这一发现，震惊了世界。中国国家文物局随即派出考古专家、文物专家进行现场考察，并决定由陕西省组织考

> Emergence of Miracle

On 11th March 1974, when a farmer was digging a water well 1 kilometres east to the Mausoleum of Qin Shihuang on a barren sandy land in Lintong County, Shaanxi Province, he found many pottery fragments, bronze arrowheads and crossbows. For generations, people of this land had found pottery figurines and the local villagers called them *Waye* (literally male figurine made of earth). Local farmers reported this finding to the government and the Bureau of Culture in Lintong County dispatched staff to the reported place and conducted protective treatment of the water well site. The staff brought back the cultural relics and after tens of days' efforts and repairing work, a few figurines of warriors were completely restored. This finding amazed the whole world. Archaeologists and experts of the National Cultural Heritage

● 农民发现"瓦爷"的地方
Site Where Farmers Discovered *Waye*

古队进行发掘。

考古队经过一年多精心的钻探和尝试性发掘，发现这是一座大型的秦朝时期的兵马俑坑。考古队将其命名为"一号俑坑"。1976年，考古人员在一号坑的左右两侧，又先后发现了二号和三号兵马俑坑。三个兵马俑坑的总面积达到了2万余平方米，共有陶俑、陶马等约8000件，整个阵势活像一个庞大的秦朝地下军团。

Administration were sent to inspect and investigate this site and it was decided that Shaanxi Province would establish a specialized archaeological team to continue this excavation.

After more than one year's careful exploration and research, this archaeological team found a large pit of terracotta warriors of the Qin Dynasty (221 B.C.-206 B.C.) and called it Terracotta Warriors Pit No.1. In 1976, archaeologists found and excavated Terracotta Warriors Pit No.2 and No.3

此后，秦始皇陵考古发现接连不断，如在秦始皇陵东侧发现了百余座马厩陪葬坑、17座陪葬墓，陵园西侧发现了31座珍禽异兽陪葬坑、一座曲尺形马厩陪葬坑和61座小型墓坑。10乘大型彩绘铜车马、木车马则位于地宫之西，原封土之下。近年来又在秦始皇陵北发现了一座较大的动物陪葬坑，在东内外城垣之间发现了铠甲坑、百戏俑坑等。

on both sides of Pit No.1 successively. The total area occupied by the three pits covers more than 20,000 square metres and contains nearly 8000 pottery figurines and horses, veritably similar to a huge underground army of Qin.

Later, the archaeological findings of this imperial mausoleum continued. For instance, hundreds of burial chambers for horse stables and 17 subordinate tombs were explored east to the mausoleum; 31 chambers for rare fowls and beasts, 1 right-angled chamber for stables and

- **修复中的秦俑**
陶俑、陶马大多是由几十甚至上百个破碎的陶片粘接修复起来的。
Pottery Figurines of the Qin Dynasty in Restoration
The pottery figurines and horses are generally repaired and spliced by tens or even hundreds of fragments.

61 small tombs were found west to the mausoleum; 10 large painted bronze and wooden chariots and horses were located to the west of the underground palace, underneath the original grave seal mound. In recent years, a relatively large tomb for animals was found north to the mausoleum and to the east, the pits for armour and acrobatics figurine between the inner and outer city walls were unearthed.

- 散落的陶片
  Pottery Fragments

> 地下军阵

秦始皇陵兵马俑坑堪称是世界上现存的最大的地下兵阵，目前发现的3个兵马俑坑坐西向东，呈"品"字形排列开来。秦始皇陵兵马俑最早被发现的是一号俑坑，其左右两侧又各有一个兵马俑坑，称二号坑和三号坑。兵马俑坑布局合理，结构独特，在深5米左右的坑底，每隔3米就会架起一道东西向的承重墙，兵马俑整齐地排列在过洞中。

兵马俑一号坑为东西向的长方形坑，长约230米，宽约62米，深约5米，总面积达到了14260平方米。一号坑的四周有斜坡门道，坑东西两端有长廊相通，南北两侧各设计一边廊，中间为九条东西向的过洞，过洞之间均以致密的夯土实墙

> Underground Troops

The Terracotta Warriors of the Mausoleum of Qin Shihuang is rated as the largest existing underground pottery troops in the world. Three unearthed pits are constructed facing to the east, forming a large "triangle" (like the Chinese character "品"). Among the three pits, the Pit No.1 is the first found pit and the other two located on both sides of it, known as Pit No.2 and Pit No.3. The overall arrangement and structure of these pits are rational and unique that in the pit bottom of approximately 5 metres deep, every 3 metres there is an east-west bearing wall, between which all pottery figurines and horses are neatly placed.

Terracotta Warriors Pit No.1 is an east-west rectangle pit, which is about 230 metres long, 62 metres wide and 5 metres deep, occupying an area up to 14,260 square metres. Around Pit

● 一号坑
Pit No.1

间隔开来。

　　一号坑以车兵为主体（车兵是春秋时期中原地区大多数国家军队中的主力兵种），步兵为辅，成矩形联合编队排列。军阵的主体向东，在南、北、西边廊中各有一排武士面向外站立着，担任阵仗的护翼和后卫。在东面，三排武士为先锋，担当前卒的角色。九个过洞内排列着战车与步兵的庞大主体军阵：每个过洞有四列武士，有的身穿厚重的铠甲，有的穿着轻盈的战

No.1 there are sloping gateways; long corridors are connected to the east and west ends and two corridors are designed and built in the south and north of the pit. The 9 east-west corridors in the middle are divided by compact walls made of rammed earth.

　　Pit No.1 mainly contains pottery chariot soldiers which were the major forces of the majority of states in Central China during the Spring and Autumn Period and Warring States Period (770 B.C.-221 B.C.), with the infantry

• 一号坑【局部】
Pit No.1 [Part]

袍，在中间配有战车，每辆战车后有驾驶车辆的士兵一名，车里面还有两名威武的军士。

二号俑坑位于一号坑的东北侧、三号坑的东侧，东西长约96米，南北宽约84米，呈曲尺形排列，总面积约为6000平方米。二号俑坑内的建筑与一号坑相同，但布阵更为复杂，兵种更为齐全。二号坑内有3个坑中最为壮观的军阵，是由骑兵、战车和步兵（包括一部

figurines as supplementary. The army is arranged into rectangles. The bulk of the array faces to the east and there is one row of warriors standing outwards in the corridors in the south, north and west serving as the safeguards and rear guards of the troops. On the east, three rows of warriors are the vanguard, performing as the pioneering soldiers. Enormous chariots and infantry arrays are in the 9 middle corridors as the main body of the troops: for every corridor there are 4 rows of warriors with some in heavy armour

分弩兵）组成的多兵种混合作战部队。二号坑目前出土有陶俑、陶马共1300多件，战车80余辆，青铜兵器数万件，其中将军俑、骑兵俑、跪姿射俑均为首次发现。二号坑东、西两端各有4个斜坡门道，北边有2个斜坡门道。

二号坑坑内的布局分为4个单元。第一单元位于俑坑东端，四周长廊有立式的弩兵俑60个，阵心由8组面向东的160个蹲跪式弩兵俑组成。弩兵采取"阵中有阵"的编列，立、跪起伏轮番射击，以保持弩兵攻击的持续性和最大范围的杀伤力。第二个单元位于俑坑的右侧，由64乘战车组成方阵，因为制作战车的材料属于木质，年代久远而腐朽，现在仅保留有战车的遗迹。战车车阵每列8乘，共有8列，车前驾有真马大小的陶马4匹。每车后一字排列兵俑3个，中间是拉马辔的战车驭手，另两个兵士分别立于车左右，手持长柄的战斗兵器，时刻准备冲击敌方战阵。第三单元位于阵仗的中部，由19辆战车、264个步兵俑和8个骑兵俑组成，共分3列，呈长方形排列。在战马方阵

and some in light battle suits. On each chariot in the corridors there is a soldier for driving and two brave and mighty warriors for fighting.

Pit No.2 is located to the northeast of Pit No.1 and the east of Pit No.3, which is approximately 96 metres long from east to west and nearly 84 metres wide from south to north in right-angled formation, occupying a total area of about 6,000 square metres. Compared with the constructions in Pit No.1, those in Pit No.2 share the same structure but enjoy a relatively more complicated arrangement with more comprehensive and complete arm forces. Pit No.2 obtains the most magnificent military forces among the 3 pits, which is a combat troop consisted of the cavalry, chariot troop and infantry (including some crossbowmen). At present, there are more than 1300 pottery figurines and horses, more than 80 chariots and tens of thousands of bronze weapons unearthed from Pit No.2, among which the general figurine, cavalry figurine and kneeling archer figurine are found for the first time. There are four sloping gateways on each side of the east and west ends in Pit No.2 and the other two are located in the north.

There are four sections in Pit No.2:

• 二号坑
Pit No.2

前面有一个骑兵俑，一手牵马缰，一手作拉弓搭箭的样子，双眼盯着前方，似乎即将投入一场惨烈的战斗。在每辆战车的后面，还有8—36个步兵俑，配合着战车进行战斗。第四单元位于军阵的左侧，由108个骑兵俑和180匹陶鞍马排成11列横

section one lies in the eastern corner of the pit. There are four corridors around the four sides where 60 crossbowman figurines are in standing posture. Totally 160 kneeling archer figurines in 8 rows facing to the east are situated in the centre of the square. All crossbowmen are arranged in "multi-level" amid whom some are standing and some are kneeling and shooting arrows, in order to maintain the attack consecutiveness and lethality made by crossbowmen to the largest extent. Section two is on the right of the pit where 64 war chariots make up a combat formation. Since the material of the chariots is wood and rots away after long periods of time, only some relics of the chariots remain. For each row there are eight chariots and totally eight rows are presented, with four real-horse-sized pottery horses drawing in the front. Three warriors are side by side behind the chariot, with the middle one grasping the bridle and driving the carriage, and the others standing on either side, holding pole weapons preparing for assaulting the enemy at any time. Section three is located in the centre of the pit, made up of 19 chariots, 264 infantry figurines as well as 8 cavalry figurines, forming three clusters in a

队，组成长方形的骑兵战阵，其中第1、第3列为战车，共有6辆。每匹马前立有胡服骑兵俑一个，右手牵马，左手也呈拉弓状。

三号俑坑位于一号坑的西北侧，与二号坑东西相对分布，南距一号坑25米，东距二号坑120米，面积约为520平方米。三号俑坑是三个俑坑中面积最小的，共出土兵马俑68个，整体呈"凹"字形排列，由南北厢房和车马房组成，车马房中有一辆驷马战车及四件兵马俑。三

rectangular combat formation. One cavalryman stands in front of a horse with one hand drawing a bow and the other hand holding the rein, staring at the front with full hostility as he is ready for a fierce fighting. Additionally, there are 8 to 36 infantry soldiers standing by each chariot in the rear to support the assault. Lying in the left of the pit, section four contains 108 cavalry figurines and 180 pottery horses ranked in 11 rows, making up a rectangular array, among which the first and third rows consist of 6 chariots

- 三号坑
Pit No.3

号俑坑虽然面积相对较小，但却是三个俑坑的核心，从三号坑的内部布局来看，应该是一、二号坑的指挥中枢。三号坑也是这三个坑中唯一没有被大火焚烧过的俑坑，出土的陶俑身上的彩绘痕迹相对明显，颜色也比较鲜艳。

秦陵兵马俑坑军阵的布局和兵种的样式，透露着一种随战场形势变化，军阵和兵种配置也随之发生变化的形态。兵俑中手执弓弩的射手射击后，可迅速分开于两侧，给后面的主力攻击部队让路；骑兵则可以根据不同的敌情，以迅疾的速度冲出军阵，冲击敌人的两翼，和

respectively. One cavalry figurine in *Hu's* (ancient Chinese tribe) suits stands in front of each horse with his right hand holding the rein and left hand in the posture of drawing a bow.

Pit No.3 is situated to the northwest of Pit No.1. With Pit No.2, they lie on the east and west directions. Pit No.3 is 25 metres south to Pit No.1, 120 metres east to Pit No.2 and occupies an area of approximately 520 square metres. As the smallest pit in area among the three, the total number of the unearthed figurines is 68, built in the shape of the Chinese character "凹", which is lower in the middle and higher on both sides, consist of two wing rooms on the south and north and one horse chamber.

- 三号坑【局部】
  Pit No.3 [Part]

• 春秋战国时期的车战
Chariot Battle of the Spring and Autumn Period and Warring States Period

步兵主力形成犄角左右夹击敌军。

秦军这种战场战术的变化是有先例的，这种阵仗在春秋中期的车战中就已出现端倪。到了战国时期，随着步兵与骑兵的兴起，这种夹击队形的阵法已被大多数作战部队所采用。春秋时期互相冲击的大规模车阵战已经过时，这种能够灵活移动、迅速追击、多变迅捷的战术成为阵仗的主流形态。这种阵法称为"雁行阵"，即兵力配置如大雁飞过的阵形，可以充分发挥弓弩兵等射击兵种的威力。攻击伤害的覆盖面较大，常常可以用来包围敌军，达到围歼敌军的目的。

Inside the horse chamber, there is a four-horse-drawn chariot and four warrior figurines. Although the total area of Pit No.3 is comparatively limited, it performs as the command centre or headquarters for all the groups in the other two pits based on the internal layout of Pit No.3. It is also the only pit free from burning and based on that, the painting on the pottery figurines unearthed from this pit is relatively more splendid and colorful.

According to the layout of terracotta warriors and the different arms and forces in the Mausoleum of Qin Shihuang, the changeable battlefield situation as well as the array and military force arrangement can be presented without reservation.

一号坑
Pit No.1

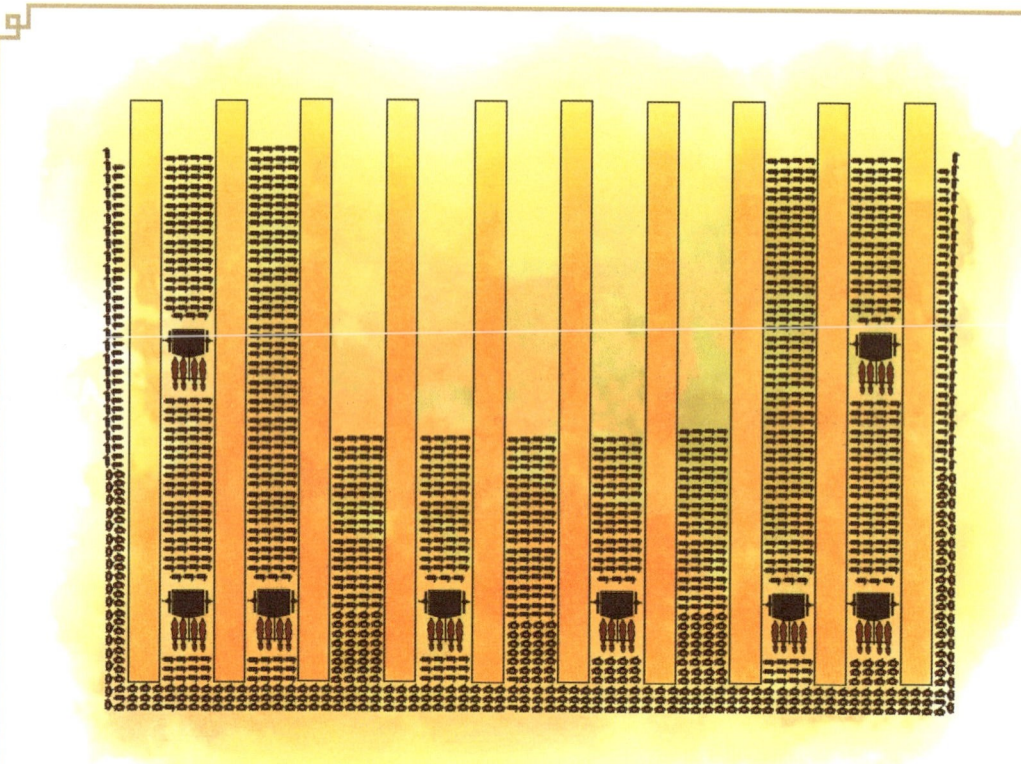

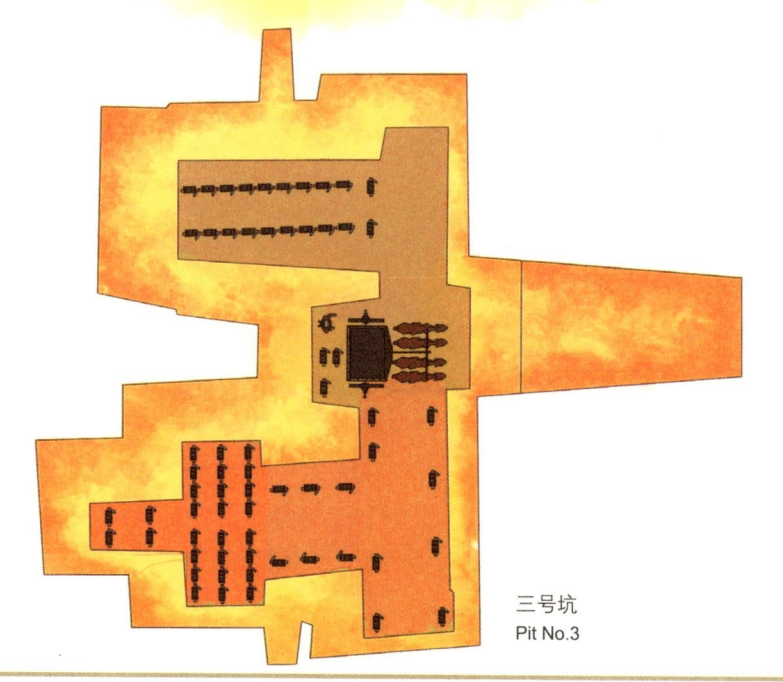

三号坑
Pit No.3

二号坑
Pit No.2

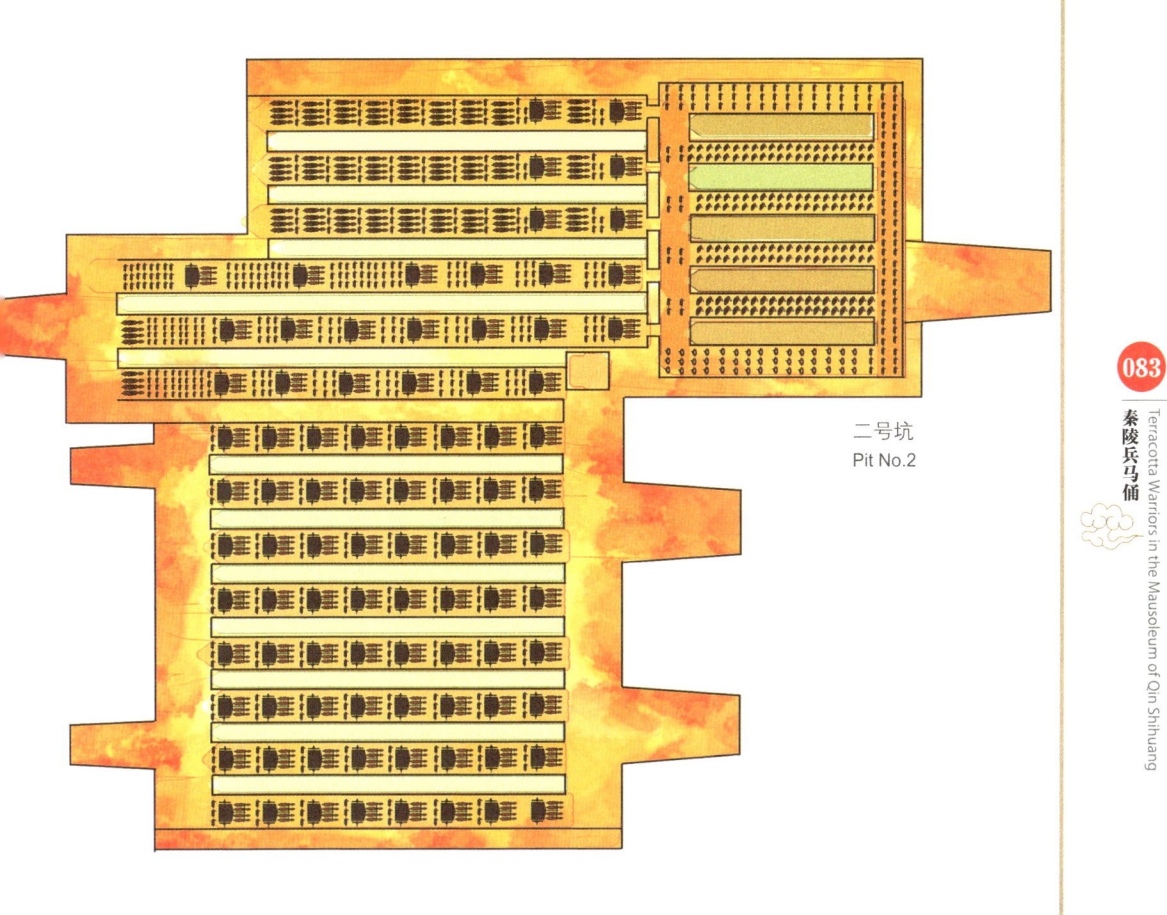

兵俑	跪射俑	战车	鞍马
Terracotta Warriors	Kneeling Archer Figurine	Chariots	Terracotta Saddled Horses

• 三坑布局图
Layout of Three Pits

从秦始皇陵兵马俑坑排列的兵阵来看，秦步兵仍然是战斗的主力部队，数量大、装备精良、作战熟练，并且远战能力较强。大规模的步兵同战车、骑兵的相互配合，在

- 秦始皇陵园里的秦代武士表演
Qin's Warrior Show Performed in the Mausoleum of Qin Shihuang

The archers in this figurine army could separate to both sides after shooting the arrows, in order to make way for the subsequent main strength of the troops; in terms of different situations, the cavalry can conduct a sudden assault on both flanks of the enemy. Cooperated with the main force, they can complete a converging attack on the enemy.

This tactics employed of Qin's troop actually first emerged during the middle of the Spring and Autumn Period. In the Warring States Period (475 B.C.-221 B.C.), with the rise of the infantry and cavalry, this converging attack had popularized in most combat troops. During the Spring and Autumn Period, the massive chariot battle had been outdated, replaced by this flexible, prompt and elastic strategy as the mainstream, known as the "goose-shaped array", meaning that the arrangement of the military force is similar to that of the geese when they fly. This strategy can help to give full play to the power of crossbow and other shooting troops. The range of lethality is relatively large and generally, this method was employed to siege the enemy.

With regards to the array arrangement of the Terracotta Warriors

- 跽坐围人俑

此俑为秦始皇陵小型马厩坑出土的男性陶俑,头绾圆髻于脑后,面目清俊,身穿交领右衽长衣,腰间束带,两腿跪地成坐姿。从面容上看,年龄较小,当为饲养马匹的仆役。

Kneeling Figurine

This pottery statue was excavated from the small pit of horse stable in the Mausoleum of Qin Shihuang. The man has bright eyes and graceful facial outline, with his hair done in a bun. He wears a robe with the front part crossing up to his chest and a belt around his waist. Based on his facial features, it can be inferred that he is in his early age and works as a servant in charge of raising the horses.

统帅的号令之下,诸兵种协同作战,形成强有力的战斗能力。

秦陵中众多的与人等高的陶俑和威武的陶马,按照军事序列和兵阵的形式排列。它们再现了秦军列

inside the pits of the Mausoleum of Qin Shihuang, the infantry played the major role in Qin's troop, with large solider numbers, superior weapons, sophisticated operations and comparatively stronger ability in distant fights. Under the unified command, with excellent cooperation among the extensive infantry, chariots and cavalry, Qin's troop formed outstanding combat ability.

The numerous pottery figurines which share the same height with real human beings and mighty horses unearthed from the mausoleum are arranged in military array and successfully reproduce the scences of real troops, camping, fighting and practical army life during the war, reflecting the well-trained and equipped troops and

• 春秋战国时期的士兵方阵
Warrior Array in the Spring and Autumn Period

阵、驻营、作战的场景，反映了秦国的兵强马壮、秦军的气吞山河和秦始皇本人运筹帷幄的帝王气概。

秦始皇陵兵马俑的出土，让2000多年后的人们目睹了威武雄壮的秦军营阵场景和栩栩如生的武士风貌。

horses, majestic and powerful military strength and the imperial momentum of Qin Shihuang.

The Terracotta Warriors imitates the magnificent scene of Qin military campsites and vividly presents the brave Qin soldiers more than 2,000 years ago.

> 各种兵俑

秦始皇兵马俑出于能工巧匠之手，制造年代据史学家们考证应该是始于公元前221年，至公元前209年结束，需要几万名熟练的工匠一起协作完成。

秦始皇陵的兵俑是一种陶俑，身材高大，一般在1.8米左右，形态各异，神情逼真，展现了秦代高超的雕塑技艺水平。兵俑基本上以现实生活为基础，通过细腻的艺术手法表现出真实武士的形态。秦俑的身份主要有士兵与军吏两类，军吏又有低级、中级、高级之分。一般士兵不戴冠，而军吏则束发戴冠，普通军吏的冠与将军的冠又有明显区别，身上的铠甲也不尽相同。纵观三个俑坑，每个陶俑的装束和神态都不一样。仅仅人物的发式就有

> Various Figurines

Terracotta Warriors were made by skilful craftsmen and according to historians' research that they were first produced in 221 B.C. and the manufacturing lasted to 209 B.C. completed by tens of thousands of sophisticated craftsmen.

The pottery figurines in the Mausoleum of Qin Shihuang generally obtain a tall and strong body of an average height of 1.8 metres. They are presented in various postures with lively facial expressions. All these reflect the outstanding

- 秦代将军装束复原图
  Picture of Restored General's Suit of the Qin Dynasty

许多种，手势也各不相同，面部的表情更是各有特色。它们一个个凝目聆听，且仪态威武，极具英雄气概，形象地再现了秦始皇"六王毕，四海一"的雄壮军容。

兵俑采用绘塑结合的方式，彩绘的特点：一是色调明快、绚烂，

- 秦代士兵装束复原图
  Picture of Restored Soldier's Suit of the Qin Dynasty

technique of sculpture making in the Qin Dynasty (221 B.C.-206 B.C.). Embedded in reality and depended on exquisite means of artistic technique, those figurines perfectly represent the real warriors. Qin warrior figurines are divided into normal soldiers and military officers, and military officers are further divided into primary, medium and senior three levels. Basically, soldiers do not wear hats and military officers bound up hair and wear hats. The hats of normal officers and the generals are considerably different, neither as their armour. Through observing the figurines in three pits, it is not hard to find out that the clothing and expressions of the statues vary as well. People will be impressed by the diversity of their various hair styles, gestures and facial expressions. In terms of their unique expressions, they all remain a fixed gaze and listen carefully, showing their composure and wisdom in a valiant posture. The heroic spirit shown by these warriors lays the foundation of Qin Shihuang's ambition and magnificent blueprint as "conquest of the other six states and unification of country".

The pottery figurine is splendid in painting colors and distinct in contrasting colors based on a combination of

二是运用强烈的对比色。秦俑的衣着以大红、大绿、粉紫、天蓝等色为主要颜色，同时十分注意衣服的装饰，领口、襟边、袖口等都有彩色的镶边，鞋口沿、靴梁上装饰着彩色的花边，鞋带、冠带也都是彩色的绦带。在绘与塑的关系上，制作秦俑的工匠注意将二者互相补充、配合，显示了绘塑结合、相得益彰的艺术效果。

painting and modelling. The clothes of the figurines are generally in bright red, green, pinkish purple and sky blue. What is more, the decorations of the clothes are special that the neckline, edge and cuff as well as the shoe topline and back strap are all decorated with colorful selvages. The shoelaces and hat strap are colorized silk braid. Craftsmen in the Qin Dynasty focused on the complementarity of painting and modelling in order to integrate these two skills to create the best artistic effect.

秦俑的制作

秦始皇陵兵马俑的制作十分复杂，为绘、塑结合，且以塑为主。大致来讲，就是先用泥塑成俑的粗胎，然后稍加修饰和刻画细部。在头、手、躯干等各部分别制作完成后，再组装成为一件完整的陶俑。

俑头一般采用合模法制成，即将俑头分为大致相等的前后两半，分别用单片模制作，然后将两片单模粘接成完整的俑头。陶俑的双耳、发髻等大多采用单模单独制作成型后，贴接于头部。头部的细部雕饰主要是五官、胡须及发纹。每个陶俑的表情都不相同，所以其面部的肌肉也是不一样的。比如神情威严者眉间的肌肉就要雕得稍稍隆起，年老者则要在额头刻画出皱纹。

陶俑躯干的塑造也是先用泥塑成粗胎，然后在粗胎上进行细部刻画，雕刻出衣纹、铠甲、腰带、带钩等。最先制作的是陶俑站立的脚踏板，用方形模具制作而成，其制作方法如今一些农村仍在使用。脚踏板制成后，就要塑造双脚，并在上面

• 兵马俑的头部
Heads of Figurines

接塑双腿和短裤。由于陶俑的腿部装束各不相同，所以在塑造时俑腿分为实心和空心两种。实心俑腿一般是将泥片折叠，反复捶打成圆柱形的泥棒，再接塑于脚上；空心腿是用卷泥片法或泥条盘筑法制成。为了体现腿部筋骨、肌肉等的变化，还要再进行细部的刮削修整。短裤即是在腿部的上段外侧拍印一周粗绳纹，再将预制的泥片包裹其上，塑成裤管。

随后要塑造的是陶俑的躯干。躯干皆为空腔，采用泥条盘筑法塑成。用泥块将俑的双腿连为一个整体，接着在上部沿周边堆泥，制成高约10厘米、厚4—8厘米的椭圆形底盘。待底盘完全阴干后，再在上面用泥条盘筑法塑造躯干。为了使盘筑的泥条接合密实，还要在内侧以麻布等编织物作为衬底，并用木槌反复锤打。

躯干塑好并完全阴干后，就可以粘接俑的双臂了。双臂亦为空心，直形臂一般用泥条盘筑法制作成型，曲形臂则要以肘部为界，分为两节分别制作。双臂粘接于躯干两侧后，为了使其接合严密，还要在粘接面采取一些措施加固，并在下端用"丁"字形木架支撑。陶俑的手是单独制成的，一般用捏塑结合制作，并刻画出指甲、关节、纹理等，最后插接在陶俑双臂袖管内。

经过以上工序，陶俑的整体躯干就塑造完成了，进一步细致雕饰后即可进行烧制。

陶俑的烧制与砖瓦陶器一样，其原料的选择和烧制都有着一定的标准。古人在选择制陶原料时，要求掘地二尺（约0.67米），取无沙的黏土。原料选好后，要经过复杂漫长的加工，才能制坯。秦俑的胎壁一般为2—4厘米厚，最厚处可达10—20厘米。泥质一般分为内、外两层，外层泥质细密均匀，内层泥质较粗，掺有白色砂粒。制作秦俑的陶土取自秦始皇陵附近的黄褐色土，经过晒干、碾轧、淘洗等一系列工序后塑造成型。为了使秦俑不会因高温而扭曲变形或膨胀炸裂，工匠们还在陶土中加入了精心筛选的石英砂粒。

陶俑烧制质量的好坏关键在于火候的掌握。温度低则烧出的成品表面无光而且内部不能烧结，温度过高则容易炸裂或变形。只有温度恰到好处（950℃—

• 兵马俑的手部
Hands of Terracotta Warriors

• 兵马俑的躯干
Figurine Bodies

1050℃）才能烧成品色纯、质坚、型正的俑来。陶俑因部位不同，胎质的厚薄也不同，相差可达十多厘米，很容易出现有些部位已烧结，而有些部位烧不透的情况。为了解决这个矛盾，工匠们将过于厚实的部位制成空心，或在内胎上堆起一道道的泥棱，从而使陶俑各部位受热均匀。为了使陶俑在烧制过程中通气流畅，工匠们还在陶俑上留有若干孔眼，比如在臀部留一两个圆孔。秦俑的烧制成功足以证明早在两千多年前的秦代，中国的制陶工艺就已达到了很高的水平。

Manufacture Process of Qin's Pottery Figurine

The manufacture process of Terracotta Warriors in the Mausoleum of Qin Shihuang is extremely complicated, mainly completed by modelling and combined with painting. The greenware of the figurine is produced in the mould, roughly decorated and carved with the details. The components like the head, hands and main body will be assembled to form a complete figurine afterwards.

  The figurine's head is manufactured through integrating two moulds, meaning that the head is produced separately in front and back. Ultimately the complete head will be finished through splicing together the two. The ears and hair buns of the figurines are generally completed in separate moulds before being assembled to the head. The five sense organs, beard and hairline are precisely carved on their faces. Since the facial expressions of each figurine vary, their facial muscle is differently presented. For instance, the majestic expression is displayed through the slight frown; the wrinkle on the forehead will help to clearly distinguish the elders from the youths.

The manufacturing of the figurine body is similar with that of the head. Craftsmen produce the greenware in the moulds firstly, followed by carving details like the grains, armour, waistband and band hook on it. By using the square mould, the firstly produced component is the foot board and this manufacturing method is still being used in some rural areas at present. After this step, the feet connected to this board will be produced. The legs and breeches will be made based on the feet. According to the differences existing in each part of the costume, the legs are produced in hollow or solid types. The solid leg is made out of folded clay slab through repeating beat and finally becomes a cylindrical clay stick, which will be attached to the foot. The hollow one is manufactured through rolling the clay slab or clay coil. In order to standing out the leg muscles and bones, the details need to be further scraped and corrected. The breeches are made through creating a circle of coarse rope grain, onto which a piece of clay slab will be attached later to form the breeches.

The figurine body will be produced after the previous steps, which is hollow and completed through rolling the clay coils. This means that craftsmen will use clay to connect the two legs to the body, followed by piling up clay around the upper part to complete an oval base plate of 10 centimetres high and 4 to 8 centimetres thick. When the base plate fully dries in the shade,

- 制作陶俑的工人模型（图片提供：FOTOE）
Model of Craftsmen Making Terracotta Figurines

the upper part will be modelled through rolling the clay coils on it. To ensure the connection tightness of the rolling clay coils, the inner side is added with lining whose material is braided fabric like the linen, and it is necessary to be repeatedly patted with mallet.

After the body is totally dried in the shade, both arms of the figurine, which are hollow, will be then added to the body. The straight arm is modelled by rolling clay coils and bending arm is divided into two parts through the elbow and manufactured separately. Two arms are attached to both sides of the body and some reinforcement measures will be taken to ensure the strict connection. In addition, the lower part of the body is supported by a "T-shaped" wooden stand. The hands of the figurines are specially manufactured through pinching and modelling. The craftsmen will assemble the hands to the arms inside the sleeves after carving the details of nails, joints and grains on the two hands.

Through all these manufacturing processes, the whole body of a pottery figurine is completed. After further carving and corrections, the figurine can be fired.

The firing of pottery figurines is the same as that of pottery tiles and utensils whose material selection and firing processes follow the certain standard. Ancient Chinese people dug the earth of two *Chi* (46.2 centimetres at that time) for the clay without any sand as the material of pottery making. After a long time of infusion, the clay can be used to make greenware. The greenware thickness of terracotta warriors is generally from 2 to 4 centimetres and the thickest place can reach 10 to 20 centimetres. The clay is made up of two levels that the outer level is fine and smooth and the inner level is relatively coarse mixed with white sand grains. The clay employed to manufacture the figurines is the yellow-brown earth from the nearby area of mausoleum. After a series of processes of drying, becking and elutriation, the clay can be used to model. The craftsmen meticulously blend quartz sand into the clay to avoid the figurines from deformation, expanding and explosion because of the high temperature.

The key of firing terracotta figurines is the temperature. If the temperature is too low, the surface of the finished products will become dim and the figurines won't be sintered inside. However, if the temperature is too high, it is quite possible for the product to burst into pieces or become out of shape during the firing process. Only when the temperature stays around 950℃ -1,050℃, can one create a solid and well shaped terracotta figurine in pure color. What is more, the different parts of an unfired figurine may have different thickness, probably up to 10 centimetres. Therefore it is highly possible to happen that some parts of the figurine are sintered while others are not. To solve this problem, the craftsmen cored out the thick sections to partly hollow the figurines, or made earthen ridges inside the unfired products to make sure that all parts can be heated evenly. Additionally, they also left ventilation holes in the figurines (i.e. one to two round holes in the buttocks) to aerate smoothly. The success of firing terracotta warriors suffices to show that even in two thousand years ago in the Qin Dynasty (221 B.C.-206 B.C.), China's ceramic technology had already achieved a significant level.

秦俑彩绘的保持

  秦陵兵马俑身上的彩绘非常特殊，有着复杂的工艺。工匠先要在烧好的陶俑上涂上一层生漆，这种生漆是从植物中提取的天然色素。然后在生漆上进行着色。

  秦俑彩绘主要有红、绿、蓝、黄、紫、褐、白、黑八种颜色。如果再加上深浅浓淡不同的颜色，如朱红、粉红、枣红色、中黄、粉紫、粉绿等，其颜色就不下十几种了。经研究人员化验表明，这些颜色均为矿物质。红色由辰砂、铅丹、赭石制成，绿色为孔雀石，蓝色为蓝铜矿，紫色为铅丹与蓝铜矿合成，褐色为褐铁矿，

- **汉代彩绘兵俑**
  图中的彩绘兵俑是距今2150多年前的西汉的第三代楚王刘戊的陪葬品，现存陶俑2393件，皆为陶土烧制，有马4匹，官吏俑1件，其余为甲胄俑、跪坐俑、盔甲俑、发辫俑、发髻俑、弓弩手俑及持长械俑等。俑身涂粉，局部绘朱。

Colored Terracotta Warriors (Han Dynasty, 206 B.C.-220 A.D.)
The colored terracotta warriors in the picture was made 2,150 years ago as funeral objects of the third emperor of State Chu (Liu Wu) in the Western Han Dynasty (206 B.C.-25 A.D.). At present there are 2,393 terracotta figurines, all made out of pottery clay, including four horse figurines, one official figurine. The rest include warrior with helmet, kneeling warrior, armored warrior, warrior with braid, warrior with chignon, crossbowman, warrior with long weapon, etc. The bodies of those figurines were painted overall in pink and partially in red.

白色为铅白和高岭土，黑色为无定形碳……这些矿物质都是中国传统绘画的主要颜料。秦俑运用了如此丰富的矿物颜料，这不仅在彩绘艺术史上堪称奇迹，而且在世界科技史上都有着重要意义。

在秦陵兵马俑刚开始发掘的时候，考古工作者就发现了陶俑身上的彩绘痕迹，但这些彩绘在空气中经过一段时间之后，就逐渐褪去了鲜艳的色彩。如何保护这些陶俑身上的彩绘成为困扰考古人员的一个重要课题。

1992年，德国巴伐利亚文物保护局与陕西省文物局就秦俑文物保护进行合作，主要合作项目中包括秦俑彩绘分析加固。随后经过不断地探索，专家们终于揭开了秦陵兵马俑彩绘的层次结构、物质组成和彩绘工艺等诸多谜团。中德专家们终于确定了两套行之有效的保护处理方法：一是用抗皱剂和加固剂联合处理的方法，即PEG200和PU联合处理法；二是单体渗透，电子束辐照聚合加固保护法。1999年，首次采用第一种方法保护了整体彩绘俑。随后，该项技术被应用于汉景帝阳陵、秦陵陪葬坑出土的彩绘陶俑的保护处理。

Maintaining the Painted Surface of Terracotta Warriors

The colored drawings on the terracotta warriors are very special, as they were not painted directly on the surface of the figurines. Instead, they were conducted with a sophisticated technological process: the craftsmen firstly painted a layer of raw lacquer that is a kind of natural pigment collected from plants on the surface of fired figurines, and then added different colors on this layer.

    The colored drawings mainly include eight colors: red, green, blue, yellow, purple, brown, white and black. If both deep and light colors are counted as well, there are actually more than ten colors, such as bright red, rosy red, purplish red, medium yellow, rosy purple, rosy green, etc. Researchers' tests show that these colors were produced out of minerals: the red color was produced from cinnabar, red lead and ocher, the green from malachite, the blue from azurite, the purple from red lead and azurite, the brown from limonite, the white from white lead and kaolin, and the black from amorphous carbon… All those minerals above are employed in traditional Chinese painting. Therefore the adoption of this rich range of mineral colors in painting terracotta warriors is not only considered a miracle master piece in the world history of colored drawing but also of great significance in the world history of technology.

    When the excavation of terracotta warriors just started, archaeological workers have found colored drawings on the unearthed figurines. However, their bright colors gradually faded after being exposed to the air for a period of time. Therefore how to protect the colored drawings has become a primary task for archaeological experts.

In 1992, the Germany-based Bavaria State Administration for Cultural Relics Protection cooperated with the Cultural Relics Bureau of Shaanxi Province to carry out some programs including analyzing and strengthening the colored drawings on unearthed terracotta warriors. Through constant research and study, experts have successfully solved puzzles of the structure, composition and painting techniques of terracotta drawings. At last Chinese and Germany experts agreed on two effective methods to protect their colors. One method is a joint treatment with anti-crease agent and reinforcement agent, namely PEG200 & PU treatment. The other method combines monomer penetration with electron beam irradiation to reinforce colors. In 1999, the PEG200 & PU treatment was employed in protecting the overall painted figurines for the first time. Then it was also used to protect the colored figurines unearthed from both Yangling Mausoleum of Emperor Jing in the Han Dynasty and pits of the Mausoleum of Qin Shihuang.

- 刚出土的兵马俑带有鲜艳的色彩（图片提供：全景正片）
Newly Unearthed Terracotta Warriors with Bright Colors

将军俑

将军俑又称"高级军吏俑",是目前俑坑中级别最高者。将军是战争中起举足轻重作用的指挥者,因此在兵马俑坑中将军数量俑屈指可数。

从出土的十数件将军俑来看,面目表情、年龄、爵位各有不同。

• 将军俑
General Figurine

General Figurine

General figurine, also called "the figurine of high-ranking army officer", is the highest-ranking figurine in all pits discovered so far. During the wartime, general was the commander who played the decisive role, therefore the number of general figurine in terracotta warrior pits is only a few.

It can be told that the dozen unearthed general figurines all have different expressions, ages and rankings. Some generals were in their thirties: their chiseled faces with full large foreheads give an air of military authority with youthful energy as well as exceptional braveness with strategic wisdom. The elder generals had a peaceful expression on their thin and bearded faces, displaying their reserved manner, moderate attitude and resourceful intelligence.

Those general figurines hold their heads up proudly in general hats with their well-built bodies in elaborate robes. If observing carefully, one can find some minor differences between these generals: there is a general crossing his hands in front of the stomach, pressing on his weapon gently, another general keeping one hand open and the other clenched, and another relaxing his arms, rubbing his right thumb with right forefinger as if he is working on

壮年者，耳大面阔，天庭饱满，眉宇飞扬，表现出血气方刚、英勇善战的猛将气质。而年老者则面庞清瘦，长须可拊，神态平和，展现出不苟言笑、稳健多谋的老将风采。

将军俑头戴鹖冠，身穿战袍，昂首挺胸，体魄魁梧。细节处，有的将军俑双手交叉于腹前，轻按兵器；有的一手伸掌，一手握拳；有的双臂自然下垂，右手的拇指与食指相捏，作掐指谋算状。工匠们在塑造将军俑时，都要在俑的额头上雕出一道道皱纹，显出这些都是久经沙场、富有长期作战经验的将领。

军吏俑

军吏俑从职位上讲低于将军俑，出土的数量较多，有中级、下级之分。从外形上看，军吏俑头戴长冠，身穿甲衣，依其装束的不同，可分为三种：第一种为身穿齐膝的长襦，外披彩色的前胸甲，下穿长裤，足登翘尖履，左手按剑，右手持物不明，神情威严肃穆；第二种为身穿彩色鱼鳞甲，左手按剑，右手持戈、矛等兵器，立于步

• 军吏俑
Military Officer Figurine

tactical planning. When craftsmen were making general figurines, they carved some wrinkles on their foreheads to show that these generals were all experienced and combat-tested.

Military Officer Figurine

Military officer figurine ranks lower than general figurine. Thus there have been relatively more being unearthed. Military officer figurines have middle and lower rankings. One can tell from what he wears

兵俑之中，神情十分威猛；第三种为不穿铠甲的轻装军吏俑，身穿长襦，下穿短裤，腿扎行縢，位于轻装步兵俑行列之中。

军吏俑除了服饰上与将军俑不同之外，精神气质上也稍有差异，其体魄一般不如将军俑魁梧，但依然较为高大。

武士俑

武士俑即普通士兵俑，平均身高约1.8米。作为军阵的主体，武士俑在兵马俑坑中出土的数量是最多的，作为主要的作战力量分布于整个军阵中。

武士俑一般身穿交领右衽长袍，外披铠甲，下身穿短裤，小腿部扎裹腿，头挽圆形发髻，足蹬短靴或方口齐头翘尖履，双臂自然下垂，右手作提弓弩状。另外，武士俑可依装束的差异分为两类，即战袍武士和铠甲武士。战袍武士俑大多分布于阵表，行动灵活，铠甲武士俑则分布于阵中。武士俑的发髻位于头顶右侧，反映了秦人尚右的习俗。交领右衽长袍属于汉服，而短靴和腰际束的革带则属于胡服

as all military officers were equipped with a kind of long stiff bonnets and armor. They are categorized into three types according to their wears: the first type wears a tunic with colored front chest armor outside, and long pants in wingtip shoes. Their expressions stay solemn, their left hands pressing on the swords and right hands holding some unidentified objects. The second type wears scale armor with the sword on the left hand and right hand holding a weapon, either a dagger-axe or a spear, and stands in the infantry array with a fierce look on the face. The third type, with no armor to battle light, wears a tunic and breeches with leg wrappings and stands in the light infantry array.

In addition to the difference in clothes, military officer figurines are also distinguished from general figurines in their look. Military officer has a smaller size compared to a general, but still big and tall, with head up with pride and shoulders squared.

Warrior Figurine

Warrior figurine, namely ordinary soldier figurine, has an average height of 1.8 metres. As the main component of an array, warrior figurines have the largest unearthed

• 武士俑
Warrior Figurine

（北方匈奴人的服饰），显示了秦代民族文化的交融。

group. They are the major combat forces, spreading across all military arrays.

Warrior figurine wears a long robe with armor equipped outside, a pair of shorts and leg wrappings. The robe has a cross collar and buttons down the left front. Simply wearing a round bun, he stands in a pair of ankle boots or square-toed shoes, with his arms relaxed and a crossbow in his right hand. In addition, warrior figurines are categorized into two types based on what they wear: warrior in robe and warrior in armor. Warriors in robes lead the arrays as they maneuver more easily, while warriors in armor just wait behind them. The warrior figurine wears their hair in a knot on the top of the head, slanted to the right, from which one tells people's belief "right rather than left" in the Qin Dynasty (221 B.C.-206 B.C.). Moreover, the warrior's long robe with a cross collar and buttons down the left front comes from traditional Han clothing, while his ankle boots and leather belt comes from traditional Hu's clothing (Hu, namely Xiongnu, an ancient tribe in northern China). The combination of these two different ethnic traditions in clothing in the Qin Dynasty has manifested the communication of ethnic cultures at that time.

铠甲

春秋以前，战士的护体设备主要是皮甲，战国时虽然出现了铁甲，但皮甲仍是重要的装备。从秦陵出土的陶制模拟铠甲来看，秦军的装备则有进一步的发展，全部都是金属札叶制成的合甲，品类完备，制作相当精密。

秦俑中普通战士装备的铠甲具有如下特点：胸部的甲片都是上片压下片，腹部的甲片则是下片压上片，这种结构便于兵士的拼杀和活动。兵士厚重的铠甲下面还垫着厚实的战袍，这样可以避免铠甲磨伤士兵的皮肤，影响作战。从胸腹正中的中线来看，所有甲片都由中间向两侧叠压，肩部甲片的组合也与胸腹部相同。在肩部、腹部和颈下周围的甲片都用连甲带连接，所有甲片上都有甲钉，其数不等，但最多不超过6枚。甲衣的长度，前后相等，都是64厘米左右，下摆一般呈圆筒形。

秦代将军和军吏的铠甲也非常有特点。胸前、背后未缀甲片，皆绘几何形彩色花纹，似以一种质地坚硬的织锦制成，也有可能是用皮革做成后绘上图案。甲衣的形状是前胸下摆呈尖角形，后背下摆呈平直形，周围留有宽边，用织锦或皮革制成，上有几何形花纹。胸部以下，背部中央和后腰等处，都缀有小型甲片。全身共有160片甲片，甲片形状为四方形。甲片的固定方法是用皮条或牛筋穿组，呈"V"形，另在两肩装有类似皮革制作的披膊，胸背及肩部等处还露出彩带结头，并钉有铆钉。可以看出，秦代的铠甲较前代已经相当完善。

20世纪80年代，在秦陵一号铜车马中出土了一件铜盾。铜盾纹饰精美、线条流畅，制作非常精良。在后来的考古发掘中，考古工作者在一辆战车上还发现了秦军使用的皮质漆盾，位于九号过洞的第二辆车的右侧，应该是车右侧配置使用的，长约60厘米，宽约40厘米，尺寸大小是一号铜车马上铜盾的两倍，因使用者级别的关系，纹饰的差别也很大。这件皮质漆盾的边栏绘制多层几何纹，线条隐约可见，色彩为红、绿、白。出土的时候，

• 秦陵出土的石质头盔
Stone Helmet Unearthed from the Mausoleum of Qin Shihuang

皮质漆盾背面朝上,因此也可看到握手部分,但它只刷了一些天然彩漆,没有细致的彩绘工艺。

Armor

Before the Spring and Autumn Period (770 B.C.-476 B.C.), soldiers only had leather armor to protect themselves. Iron armor firstly appeared in the Warring States Period (475 B.C.-221 B.C.), while leather armor was still important equipment in battles at that time. According to the terracotta armor unearthed from the Mausoleum of Qin Shihuang, the army of State Qin has greatly improved their equipment, all armed with well-made iron armor composed of metal plates in a complete range.

Armor on ordinary terracotta soldiers is featured as follows: the chest plates covered the next downwards while all chips at waist level cover the next upwards. This structure provided greater flexibility for the soldiers to fight and move. Under the heavy armor the soldier wore a robe, which was thick and firm enough to protect the soldier from abrasion hence ensuring a better focus on the battle. Looking from the central chest line, all chips covered the next outwards and the construction of shoulder plates is similar to chest and stomach. All plates on the shoulder, waist and neck were connected with leather bands and decorated with a maximum six pitons each. The length of armor was equal at front and back, both 64 centimetres, with the lower edges shaped round.

The armor on generals and military officers in the Qin Dynasty (221 B.C.-206 B.C.) was also really something. There were pieces of hard brocade, or could possibly be leather, with colored geometric patterns on chest and back, rather than metal plates. Small chips were decorated below the chest, in the middle of the back as well as the back waist. The armor was crafted with triangle hem in the front and straight hem at back, where pieces of brocade or leather with geometric patterns were widely hemmed. The whole armor had 160 square plates in total, fixed in groups with leather bands or tendons, assembling a V-pattern. It also had shoulder pads with revealed colored ribbon knots and decorated pitons. Thus compared to its previous generation, the armor used in the Qin Dynasty has been absolutely perfected.

In the 1980s, a bronze shield was unearthed

• 秦陵出土的石质铠甲
Stone Armor Unearthed from the Mausoleum of Qin Shihuang

from Pit No.1, namely the bronzes chariots and horses pit of the Mausoleum of Qin Shihuang. The shield was finely crafted with sophisticated decorations and sleek curves. During the following excavations, archeologists discovered a leather shield used by the Qin soldiers on a chariot. The chariot sits the second in the 9th corridor and on its right side placed the shield and the shield is therefore believed to be a chariot shield. It is 60 centimetres long and 40 centimetres wide, twice bigger than a bronze shield placed on the first bronze chariot. There is also a big difference between their decorations due to their owners' different rankings. This painted leather shield has layers of geometric patterns decorated on the edges with blurred lines in red, green and white. It was unearthed back side up, so its handle was exposed to the air when it was discovered. Archeologists found that the handle had been painted only with natural pigments instead of being meticulously processed with drawing techniques.

盾握
Shield's Handle

盾背
Shield's Back

- **秦代铜盾示意图**

春秋战国至秦代的盾分为步兵用盾和车兵用盾。步兵盾形制较大，可防箭和维持阵列；车兵盾短而窄，利于在车上使用。盾除表面蒙有多层皮革外，还常钉有铁钉等其他金属装饰，用以增加强度。手握部位因为战斗需要而做得特别坚实、牢固。

Copper Shield (Qin Dynasty, 221 B.C.-206 B.C.)

Shields used in the Spring and Autumn Period (770 B.C.-476 B.C.) and the Warring States Period (475 B.C.-221 B.C.) down to the Qin Dynasty are categorized into infantry shields and chariot shields. An infantry shield has bigger size to block arrows and maintain combat formation, while a chariot shield is shorter and narrower, mainly used on chariots. In addition to layers of leather on the surface, shields were made with metal decorations (i.e. iron pitons) to enhance its intensity. Handles were also made strong enough for fierce battles.

立射俑与跪射俑

立射俑在秦俑中是一个较为特殊的兵种，目前共发现172件，武器皆为弓弩，与跪射俑一起组成弩兵军阵，是二号坑的前锋。立射俑位于阵表，身着轻装战袍，束发挽髻，腰系革带，脚蹬方口翘尖履，装束较为轻便灵活。这说明秦代时射击的技艺已发展到很高的水平，具有一套规范严谨的模式。

兵俑的普遍造型是立正姿势，

- 立射俑
  Standing Archer Figurine

Standing Archer Figurine and Kneeling Archer Figurine

Standing archer figurine is quite special among all types of terracotta warriors. There are 172 pieces unearthed so far, all holding crossbows. Both standing and kneeling archer figurines are front troop members in Pit No.2, together called the archer array. The archer figurine stands in the front and wears lightweight robe with hair braided in a knot on the top of his head. It also wears a pair of square-toed shoes with belt buckled around his waist. In light clothes, the archer would be more flexible. This figurine is a good proof of Chinese soldier's great shooting level in the Qin Dynasty (221 B.C.-206 B.C.), which followed a standard and strict pattern.

Most soldier figurines stand upright with relatively small movement ranges, while the standing archer figurine is a real depiction of a soldier in battle: he slightly tilted his head and twitched his lips tight, standing with arms open and legs straddled. The face was made lifelike with piercing eyes and a serious look. This type of figurine is not commonly seen in the Chinese history of sculpture, from which one can tell China's sculpture art has already achieved quite a level in

身体左右均衡对称，动作幅度较小；而立射俑则是动态的写实，头微转，嘴角绷着，略鼓着劲儿，拉开的双臂和叉开的双腿上下呼应，双目炯炯有神，表情严肃认真。这在中国古代雕塑史上较为少见，反映出两千多年前的中国的雕塑艺术已达到相当高的水平。

跪射俑目前共发现160件，所持武器亦为弓弩，在弩兵军阵中位于阵心。他们身穿战袍，外披铠甲，发髻挽于头顶左侧，脚蹬方口齐头翘尖履，左腿蹲曲，右膝着地，上体微向左侧转，双手皆位于身体右侧，一上一下作握弓状，双目凝视左前方。这是典型的弓兵操练动作。跪射俑是秦俑中唯一可以看到鞋底的，那疏密有致的花纹被工匠细致地刻画出来，十分写实。

武士俑的发髻挽于头顶右侧，而立射俑和跪射俑则挽于左侧，这是方便作战时右手抽拔箭支的真实写照。

骑兵俑

在二号俑坑内共发现了100多件陶质鞍马，且每匹马前均立有一个

• 跪射俑
Kneeling Archer Figurine

more than two thousand years ago.

There are 160 kneeling archer figurines discovered so far, all holding crossbows and placed in the centre of arrays. Dressed in robe and armor, a kneeling archer wore his bud slanted to the left. He also wore square-toed shoes, kneeling on one knee with the upper body slightly turning to the left. Looking into the left front, he held his weapon with both hands by the right side, one hand up in the front and the other down at waist level, which was a typical posture during

骑兵俑。骑兵在古代被称为"离合之兵",如鸟散云合,阵形变化多端,且可日行千里,出入无间。公元前260年,在秦、赵两国的长平之战中,秦国以骑兵5000突然插入赵军之中,使赵军一分为二,粮道被断绝,几乎全军覆灭。

这些骑兵俑的装束与普通的武士俑有着明显的不同。他们头戴圆形小帽,帽子的两侧带扣紧系在领下,身着紧袖,交领右衽双襟掩于

• 骑兵俑
Cavalry Figurine

army practice time. Kneeling archer figurine is the only figurine that shows the sole of his shoe, on which craftsmen have finely carved knitted stitches with natural density.

The warrior figurine wears its bun to the right, while both standing and kneeling archer wear their buns to the left, so that it would be easier for them to pull the arrows with their right hands in battles.

Cavalry Figurine

There are over one hundred terracotta saddled horses in Pit No.2, each with one cavalry soldier standing in front. In ancient China, cavalry was called the troop with speedy flexibility, as its flexibility and speed could make the troop change its formation as quickly as bird and cloud. This troop could cover a thousand *Li* (*Li*, ancient Chinese measurement, equals 500 metres) in a single day and reach anywhere with great ease. During the battle of Changping in 260 B.C., State Qin sent its 5,000 cavalry to attack State Zhao's army, which was split into two by this sudden attack with its supply lines cut as well. Zhao's army were almost completely annihilated.

胸前的上衣，下穿紧口连裆长裤，足蹬短靴，身披简短的铠甲，肩部无披膊装束，手部亦无护甲。这种装束是根据骑兵的战术特点而设计的。因为骑兵在作战时需要迅猛、出其不意地攻击敌人或抵御突如其来的攻击，所以要求骑兵行动敏捷，穿着自由轻便，以便自由地抬足跨马、挎弓射箭。如果骑兵身穿重铠或宽大的长袍，显然违背了骑兵的战术特点。兵马俑坑中的骑兵军阵是现实军阵的艺术再现。每个骑兵的身高都在1.80米以上，且体型修长匀称，神态机敏灵活，抬头挺胸，目视前方，造型生动传神。

驭手俑

秦始皇拥有战车千乘、战马万匹、步兵百余万，他凭借这支强大的武装力量统一了六国。在中国古代战争中，战车的杀伤力极强，且如果一辆车乱了阵脚，则必会影响阵形。所以驭手在战争中的地位十分重要，甚至直接影响着战争的胜负。秦代驭手的选拔是十分严格的，要求年龄在40岁以下，身高1.73米以上，行动要敏捷，力量要大，

The clothes of cavalry troop obviously differed from what ordinary warriors wore. A cavalry soldier had a small round hat, with strings on both sides going under his chin. He also wore a tunic with cross collar and buttons down the right front, with tight sleeves, long and tight slit-pants, as well as a pair of ankle boots. His armor was simple and short with no shoulder pad or hand guard. This was a design exclusively made based on the characteristics of cavalry soldiers: when battling, the cavalry troop needed to move fast and unexpectedly, and also fight under sudden attacks. Therefore, they needed to wear light suits in order to battle on horses and to fire arrows without difficulty. Heavy clothes, such as heavy armor or a loose robe would definitely hinder the soldier's movements when he was fighting on a horse. The cavalry array in the pit copies the real array in an artistic and lifelike way: with an average height of 1.8 metres, the cavalry soldier figurines were made slender and shapely. They all keep heads up and eyes looking straight ahead, posing vividly.

Charioteer Figurine

Qin Shihuang had thousands of

且要经过四年训练才能上战场，如果经过训练仍无法自如驾车，则免职，并补服四年徭役。

在三个坑中，共发现有战车一百多辆，包括一般战车、指挥车、佐车、驷乘车等。驭手俑又称"御手俑"，是驾驶战车的士兵俑，三个坑中均有出土。他们身穿长襦，外披铠甲，臂甲长及腕部，手部戴有护手甲，胫部着护腿，脖子上围有颈甲，头上带有巾帻及长冠，双臂前举作牵拉辔绳的驾车姿势。

• 驭手俑
Charioteer Figurine

chariots, tens of thousands of horses and over one million infantrymen, with which he unified the six kingdoms. In China's ancient wars, the chariot was a devastating presence. If one chariot lost its focus, it would affect the overall combat formation. Therefore charioteers were significantly important during the wars, and their performance would even directly influence the result. The selection of charioteers in the Qin Dynasty (221 B.C.-206 B.C.) followed strict process: the candidates must be under the age of 40 and with a height over 1.73 metres. They must be quick and of great strength. Before being sent to the battle field, they were firstly trained for four years. If they still failed to meet the standard after the four-year training, they would be fired and sent to other places as conscript labors and work for another four years.

There are over one hundred chariots discovered in all three terracotta warrior pits, including ordinary chariots, command chariots, assistant chariots, heavy chariots, etc. Charioteer figurines, also called coachman figurines, were put in charge of driving chariots in wars and therefore found in all three pits. A charioteer was dressed in a long jacket with armor covered until wrists. Equipped

文官俑

既然秦陵是秦都咸阳的缩影，就应该有朝廷的象征——文官的存在。在秦陵南部距封土20米处有一个文官俑坑，考古人员称之为"六号坑"。

文官俑的形象比较特殊，一个个头戴长冠，冠带系于颌下，带尾系成蝴蝶结。它们身穿襦裙，腰部束革带，下身穿长裤，脚穿齐头方

with hand guard, leg guard and neck guard, he also wore a Chinese turban and a long stiff bonnet on his head. The figurine lifts his arms as if he is pulling the bridle ropes to drive the chariot.

Civil Official Figurine

The Mausoleum of Qin Shihuang was built as a copy of Xianyang, the capital city of State Qin, therefore it also symbolizes the Qin court with civil officials around 20 metres south to the seal mound there is a civil called Pit No.6.

A civil official was dressed differently. He wore a long and stiff bonnet with strings tied down his chin into a bow, and a slim jacket and long pants and a pair of squared-toed shoes with low-cut uppers. The figurines are smiling in a cautious way with their eyes looking down. Some figurines have knives hanging on the waist. This is because that in the Qin Dynasty (221 B.C.-206 B.C.), people used bamboo slips to keep things down. If one made a mistake, one needed to scrape away

- 文官俑
Civil Official Figurine

口浅履。文官俑的面部表情十分恭谨，但却又带着一丝笑容，双目下垂。有些文官俑的腰部还悬挂着削，即小刀。这是因为秦代的字都是刻在竹片上的，如果写错了，就要用削刮掉重写。

百戏俑

兵马俑坑中还有一座百戏俑坑，考古人员在这里发掘出了几件

the mistake with a small knife and then recarve it.

Acrobatics Figurine

There is also a pit where a few acrobatics figurines have been unearthed. *Baixi* (*Bai*, one hundred; *Xi*, acrobatics) refers to acrobatic shows in ancient China including carrying cauldrons, wrestling, monologue, sword swallowing, pole climbing and loong-lantern show, which

- 百戏俑
Acrobatics Figurine

百戏俑。所谓百戏，是中国古代的乐舞杂技等民间游艺的统称，包括扛鼎（举鼎）、角力（摔跤）、俳优、吞刀、爬杆、耍龙灯等，在秦汉时期十分盛行，是宫廷中的主要娱乐节目。

百戏俑坑平面呈"凸"字形，坑体东西长40米，西端宽16米，东端宽12.3米，该陪葬坑总面积约800平方米。百戏俑的装束较为特别，一般腰间只系着彩色短裙，其他部位均裸露，肤色以粉色为主。百戏俑的身材差异较大，举止、神态各异，滑稽可笑。有的纤巧瘦弱，有的魁伟健壮；有的像是持竿者，有的如同角斗士；有的还有"啤酒肚"，呈现出明显的百戏特色，透着一股鲜活灵动的气息。

其中出土的一件陶俑非常奇特，是一件巨人俑。这件陶俑虽遗失了头部，但仍显得非常魁梧。这件巨人俑的身高达到了220厘米，脚长有32厘米，如果算上遗失的头部，这个陶俑身高可达250厘米，堪称巨人。

have been prevailing in the Qin Dynasty (221 B.C.-206 B.C.) and the Han Dynasty (206 B.C.-220 A.C.). *Baixi* was also the main entertainment within the imperial palace.

The acrobatics pit is bulging in the middle, with a plane structure resembling the Chinese character 凸. It is 40 metres from west to east, 16 metres wide in the west and 12.3 metres wide in the east, with a total coverage of 800 square metres. Acrobatics figurines are dressed specially: their whole pink bodies are naked except for the short colorful skirts at the waist level. They have different sizes and funny looks: some are very slim while some are very strong; some look like pole performers while some look like gladiators. There is one figurine even with a beer belly. The acrobatics figurines lively depict what *Baixi* was like in ancient times and bring a fun and fresh air to the mausoleum.

Among all acrobatics figurines, there was one standing out for its extraordinary size, namely the giant figurine. Although its head is missing, it is still abnormally big and tall. With a pair of 32 centimetres long feet, it is 220 centimetres high. After adding its head, it may reach 250 centimetres, such a giant.

秦陵中的其他陪葬品
Other Funeral Objects in the Mausoleum of Qin Shihuang

兵马俑坑只是秦陵东1.5千米处的狭小地域而已。除了兵马俑，秦始皇陵还出土了数万件陪葬品，主要包括铜车马、兵器、铜水禽等。

Not limited to the narrow area of Terracotta Warriors pits located 1.5 kilometres to the east of Mausoleum of Qin Shihuang, there are tens of thousands of funeral objects unearthed from this imperial tomb, mainly including bronze chariots and horses, ancient weapons, bronze waterfowls, etc.

> 铜车马

20世纪80年代，秦陵兵马俑坑中出土了两辆大型的彩绘铜车马，称为"一号铜车马"和"二号铜车马"，这是迄今为止中国发现的体型最为庞大、装饰最为华丽、结构最为逼真、构造最为完整的古代铜车马，被考古界誉为"青铜之冠"。这两辆举世瞩目的铜车马出土于秦始皇陵西侧20米处，作为陪葬品成为秦陵的一部分。

当时，考古人员在局部试掘铜车马坑时，在一个木制的椁内出土了一前一后纵置的两乘大型铜车马。出土时，这些铜车马早已残破不堪，后经精心的修复，恢复了铜车马的原状。铜车马华丽非常，通体彩绘，马为白驹，彩绘时所用的颜料均为用胶调和的天然矿物染

> Bronze Chariots and Horses

In the 1980s, two large color-painted bronze chariots and horses were unearthed from one pit of Terracotta Warriors, known as the No.1 and No.2 bronze chariots. So far, they are the largest ancient bronze chariots and horses in China, which is the most similar to the real chariots in structure, with the most magnificent ornaments and completed construction, enjoying the reputation "Best Bronze Ware" in archaeology. These famous bronze chariots and horses were excavated 20 metres west to the Mausoleum of Qin Shihuang as a part of the Emperor's funeral objects.

When archaeologists tried to partially dig in the pit, they found two large bronze chariots and horses encased in a large wooden coffin and excavated them successively. These bronze chariots and horses had been seriously damaged when they were dug from the pit and after meticulous restoration, they were then successfully restored. Drawn by white horses, the whole chariot is painted with natural mineral dyes mixed with glue, making this piece of art gorgeous enough. The craftsmen even took advantage of the denseness of glue to highlight the chariot's outline. As a sacrificial vessel, the bronze chariots and horses do not obtain practical functions and their sizes are just half of the scale of real ones. Since it was elaborately manufactured by a complete reference to the real chariot, the bronze chariot perfectly demonstrates the elegant demeanour of Qin Shihuang's royal parade.

The model of these two bronze chariots and horses is a luxurious chariot with canopy in the Qin Dynasty (221 B.C.-206 B.C.) and the carriage is close to square. The carriage of No.2 chariot is equipped with a turtle-shell-shaped canopy. This huge canopy covers up the whole carriage as well as the charioteer seat in front,

- 一号铜车马
No.1 Bronze Chariot

料，并且还利用胶的稠度塑造出立体的线条。铜车马是作为陪葬的礼器而存在，并不具备真实的骑乘功能，其大小为真实车辆的二分之一。铜车马是完全仿照实物精心制作完成，真实地再现了秦始皇銮驾车队的风采。

• 二号铜车马
No.2 Bronze Chariot

这两辆铜车马是仿照秦代一种带有篷盖的豪华车辆而造，车舆接近于正方形。二号铜车马上还罩着一个类似于龟盖状的篷盖。巨大的篷盖不仅将车舆全部罩了起来，甚至连车舆前边的驭手座位也有效地遮盖住了，形成了半封闭式的车舆。这种半封闭式的结构，一则便于车主向驭手传递命令和看清路况，二则可以遮挡烈日和雨雪，最大限度地保障了乘车人的舒适感。二号铜车属于后世"小轿车"样的舒适类型，车内的设备极具特色，车舆内设置了彩绘的"软垫"，车主可以坐乘，也可以在平坦的路上卧着休息片刻。

铜车马的铸造水平高超，主体为青铜构造，一些零部件为金银所铸。各个部件均是事先按照固定的尺寸铸造好，待各种零部件齐备之后，进行嵌铸、焊接、粘接、铆接、子母扣接、纽环扣接和销钉连接等，这样，众多的部件就组装成一件完成的铜车马。当时没有车床和现代化的冶铸设备，靠手工劳作和简单的机械，铸造出如此精美的大小规格不同的车马部件实在是一项伟大的工程，让人不得不佩服秦朝匠人们高超的技艺。

forming a semi-enclosed compartment. This design facilitates the people in the carriage to deliver messages to the charioteer and provides the charioteer with a sweeping view; in addition, it can protect from harsh sun, heavy rain and snow, maximizing the internal degree of comfort. The No.2 chariot can be somewhat compared with the later "saloon car" since the facility inside is very peculiar with painted "cushions" and people can sit and even lie on the cushions when the road condition allows.

The casting technique of the bronze chariot is considerably advanced that its main body is made by bronze with some gold and silver components. All components were manufactured in advance according to fixed sizes and standards, and these large amounts of components would be assembled into a complete bronze chariot based on full preparation of all parts and through applying several connecting techniques like insert casting, welding, adhesion, riveting, snap connection, buckle connection and pin seal. Without modern lathes or smelting and casting equipments, depending on manual work and simple tools alone, the accomplishment of such an exquisite and splendid project, especially for the manufacturing of the components in different sizes, deserves the highest praise

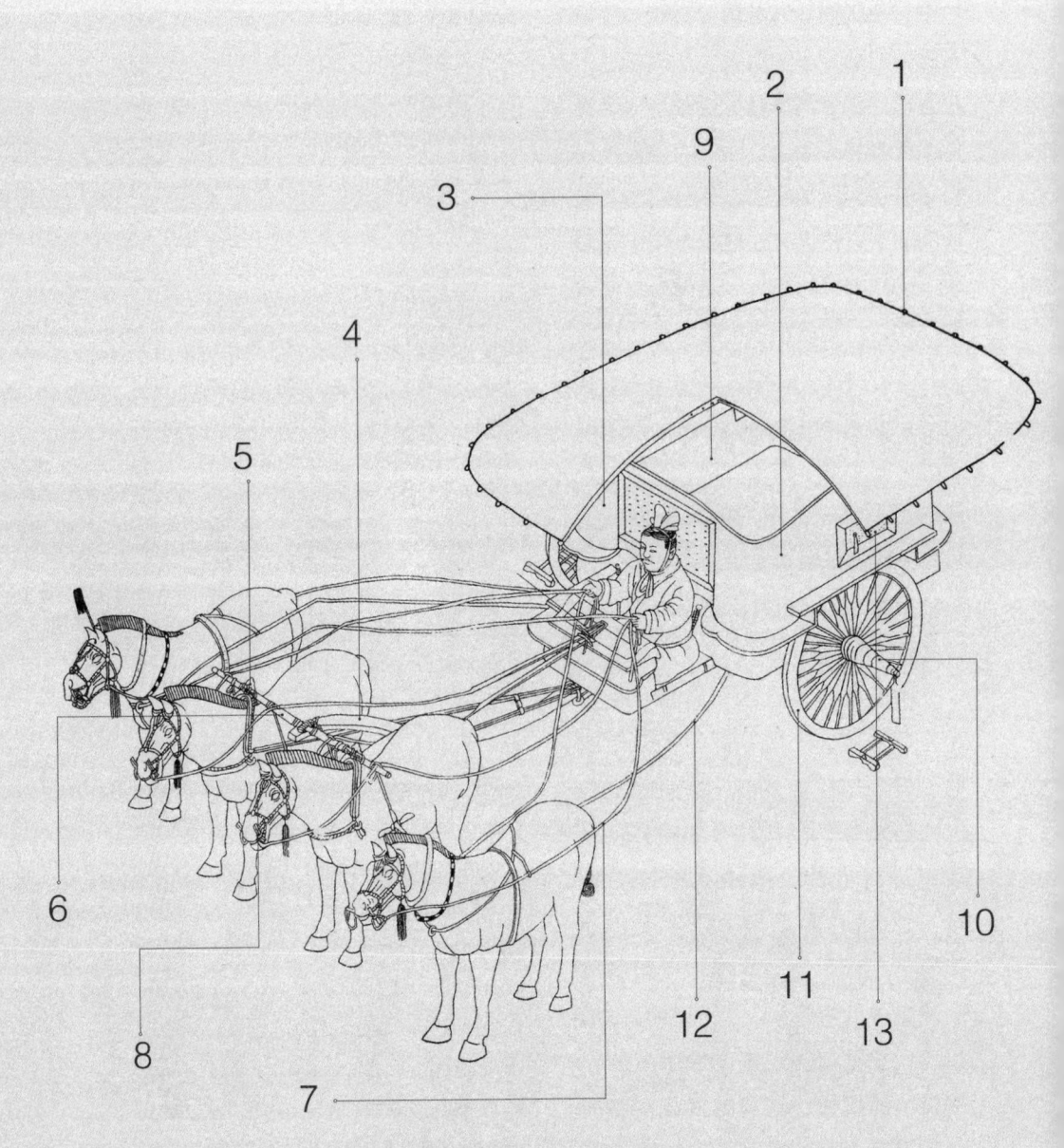

二号铜车马结构示意图
Structure Diagram of No. 2 Bronze Chariot and Horses

1.篷盖：车舆上覆以穹窿形篷盖，面积达2.3平方米，将前后两室罩在下面。篷盖下有鱼脊形的铜骨架，以脊为中心对称排列着36根圆柱形的盖弓，盖弓端套有弓帽。为了防止篷盖滑脱，弓帽上制有倒钩，将篷盖边沿紧紧钩住。

Canopy: The carriage is covered with an arched canopy of 2.3 square metres, shading the two compartments. The backbone of the canopy's bronze herringbone framework divides the frame into two symmetrical parts, with each part consisted of 36 cylindrical ribs. The ribs are connected with caps. To avoid slipping, the caps are added with hooks firmly linked to the rim of the canopy.

....

2.舆：舆分前、后两室，其平面呈"凸"字形。

Carriage: The carriage is divided into the front and the rear compartments, with a plane structure resembling the Chinese character "凸".

....

3.前室：前室为御者所居之处，底部四周有轸，4个轸之间的铜板上铸有斜方格的皮条编织纹。正面铸出正方格纹，并涂以朱漆。前室除后面以外皆立有阑板，阑板上端又有外折的车沿。前室的右后方立有一圆柱，可加固舆底，并可作为御手登车时的把手。

Front Compartment: The front compartment is for the charioteer and there are four wooden bumpers around the bottom. The bronze plate in the space formed by the four wooden bumpers is cast in woven grain of diamond checks. The front side is decorated with cast square checks, painted with red lacquer. Except the back side, the other sides of this compartment are equipped with diaphragm plates whose upper end stretching outward to form a fringe. There is a cylinder standing on the right back of the front compartment, which can strengthen the bottom, used as the handle for the charioteer to get on the carriage.

....

4.辕：辕长246厘米，前端上翘呈弓状，辕首与衡交叉成"十"字形，辕后端置于车轴上。

Shaft: The shaft is 246 centimetres long with its arciform front end cocking up. The shaft head and horizontal drawbar intersect and form a "cross". The shaft end is on the axle.

....

5.轭：轭呈鞍桥形，驾在马的颈部。轭的内侧铸有类似皮质的柔软衬垫，可防止轭磨破马颈，同时能增强轭的拽车能力。

Yoke: The yoke is saddle-shaped and set on the horse neck. The inner side of the yoke is added with soft pads whose material is similar to leather in order to prevent the horse neck from injury resulted from frequent rub. At the same time, this design can also increase the yoke's drag capability.

....

6.衡：衡长79厘米，近似圆柱形，中间较粗，其上共有5个半环形的银质纽鼻。衡与辕的交叉处正处在第三个纽鼻处。辕端有一革带穿出纽鼻，将辕与衡紧紧地缚住。

Horizontal Drawbar: The horizontal drawbar is 79 centimetres long and its shape is close to cylinder. On its relatively thicker central part there are 5 semicircular silver link knobs (fixed semi-rings). The horizontal drawbar and shaft intersect on the third link knob and they are tightly bound by one strap through a link knob on one end of the shaft.

....

7.辔绳：辔绳是马车转弯时的必要工具。四匹马各有两条辔绳，车在旋转时御者可通过拽扯不同的辔绳来控制方向。

Rein: The rein is an indispensable tool for swerving the chariot. Every horse of the four is tied with two reins and the charioteer can decide the direction through controlling the reins.

8.络头：络头由金银节组成，各有一个树叶形的金质当卢位于马面中央。两件金泡位于马口角两侧，三件银泡一件位于鼻梁正中，两件位于两颊。

Bridle: The horse bridle is made up of gold and silver joints and each horse is decorated with leaf shaped gold *Danglu* (an ornament for chariot-driving horse) on the middle of the horse face; two *Jinpao* (a round gold ornament for horse) decorate both sides of the horse month and one of the three *Yinpao* (a round silver ornament for horse) is placed in the middle of the horse nose while the other two on horse cheek.

9.后室：后室周围有厢板，分上下两层。下层为主体，呈"凸"字形，上部呈"凹"字形。上层两侧下方各有一周外翻的折沿，恰好盖住了车轮，既美观，又可在行进中遮挡泥土。

Rear Compartment: Around the rear compartment there are carriage boards and is divided into two levels. The "凸" shaped lower level is the main part and the upper level is "凹" shaped. Both sides of the upper level extend outward, which shelter the wheels from dirt during journey and beautify the whole chariot.

10.轴：轴为圆柱形，两端渐渐收成纺锤形。

Axle: The axle is cylindrical, with its two ends forming a fusiform stick.

11.轮：两轮直径均为59厘米，每轮各有30根辐条，左轮重23.7千克，右轮重23.4千克。

Wheel: The average diameter of the two wheels is 59 centimetres and each wheel owns 30 spokes. The left wheel is 23.7 kilograms and the right one is 23.4 kilograms.

12.靷绳：靷绳是牵引马匹前行的必要工具，因此四匹马均有一条靷绳。

Pulling Strap: The pulling strap is a necessary tool to drag horses. Each horse of the four is equipped with one strap.

13.窗：后室的正前和左右两侧共有三面车窗。正前的窗板上有镂空的菱形花纹，可通风采光。左、右两侧的车窗形制相同，窗板内外各有一个拉手，可前后推拉，开关灵活。

Window: There are three windows in the rear compartment, one in the front and the other two on left and right sides. The front window is decorated with hollowed-out diamond checks' pattern for ventilation and daylight. The side windows share the same structure and shape, all equipped with handles in and out of the window which facilitates opening and closing.

二号铜车马出土时破碎为1555块，经修复，恢复了较为完整的形体。二号铜车马车通长3.17米，高1.06米，总重量为1241千克，由大小3462个零部件组装而成。其中，青铜制件1742个，黄金制件737个，白银制件983个。两乘车的零部件加起来不少于5000个。而这5000多个零部件无论是大至2平方米以上的篷盖、伞盖、车舆、铜马、铜俑等，还是不足0.8平方厘米的零部件，都是一次铸造成型。铜车马的篷盖与伞盖，厚的地方为0.4厘米，薄的地

and admiration as an outstanding fruit of ancient Chinese people's wisdom.

The No.2 bronze chariot was in 1,555 pieces when excavated from the pit. After restoration, the body of the chariot is generally recuperated. This bronze chariot is 3.17 metres long, 1.06 metres tall and obtains a total weight of 1,241 kilograms, consisted of 3,462 components, among which 1,742 pieces are made of bronze, 737 of gold and 983 of silver. There are more than 5,000 components in total, including the large parts like the canopy, umbrella, carriage, bronze horses and bronze figurine that are larger than 2 square metres and

• 秦国战车示意图
Sketch of Qin's Chariot

方仅有0.1厘米，篷盖、伞盖都有一定的弧度，但却能一次性浇铸成功。而且两辆铜车马的8匹铜马、2个御官俑的铸造都达到了相当精妙的程度。铜车马对细节的构造和处理也让人叹为观止。铜马的笼头由82节小金管和78节小银管连接起来。每节扁状管长度仅0.8厘米，一节金管与一节银管以子母卯形式相连。特别值得一提的是铜车马马脖子下悬挂的璎珞，这些璎珞采用一根根细如发丝的铜丝制作而成，浑然一体，粗细均匀，秦人工匠这种高超的技艺让后世惊诧。

those small ones which occupy less than 0.8 square centimetres are all produced at one time. It is amazing that although the thickness of the canopy and umbrella vary from the thicker part of 0.4 centimetres to the thinner part of only 0.1 centimetres, combined with their slightly curved shape, the craftsmen could complete them with only one casting time. Furthermore, the 8 bronze horses and 2 figurines of charioteers are extremely delicately presented. In terms of the bronze horses, all bridles are constituted of and connected by 82 gold and 78 silver tubes revealing the breathtaking details of the structure and craft. Each flat tube is only 0.8 centimetres long and a gold tube is linked with a silver tube through mortise-and-tenon connection. It is especially worth mentioning that the silk cord wearing on the bronze horses' necks is made out of cooper wires as thin as hairlines shown as an integral whole. The harmonious and uniform thickness of each copper wire demonstrates the extraordinary and ingenious technique of the Qin craftsmen.

> 兵器

在秦陵的考古发掘过程中，考古学者们除发现了举世瞩目的兵马俑外，还发现了一批极具考古价值的秦代兵器。从出土的兵器来看，秦军武器装备显示了新旧结合、新旧交替的历史特点。

在出土的秦军武器中，有很多是当时先进的远射武器。秦陵兵马俑的出土情况表明，步兵、骑兵或车兵都装备有大量的弓弩和箭矢，就连战车上的甲士也备有弓箭。规模宏大的一号俑坑，每个步兵几乎都"背负矢箙（箭袋），手持弓弩"，二号俑坑还专门配备了一个弩兵队列。骑兵并不是手握马刀，而是一手牵马缰，一手作提弓状，配备的主要兵器其实都是弓箭。这些情况说明，弓、弩、箭是秦军最

> Ancient Weapon

Besides Terra Cotta Warriors, many other archaeologically valuable weapons have been found in the excavation process of Mausoleum of Qin Shihuang. In terms of those unearthed weapons, weapons of the Qin Dynasty (221 B.C.-206 B.C.) obtain the characteristics in this industry of old and new dynasties.

Among the unearthed weapons, advanced standoff weapons occupy a certain percentage. It is reasonable to speculate that the infantry, cavalry, chariot soldiers and even the armoured soldiers on the chariots of Qin's troop were equipped with large amounts of bows, crossbows and arrows according to the excavation of Terracotta Warriors. For the figurines, almost the whole infantry are "carrying arrow cases and holding bows and crossbows" in the large-scaled Terracotta Warriors Pit No.1; there is an

• 秦陵中出土的铜弩机
Bronze Crossbow Unearthed from the Mausoleum of Qin Shihuang

主要的武器之一。

就发掘出的秦陵弓弩来看，秦军的弓弩主要分为大、小两种——小弓弩主要是近距离射杀，射程为150米，射击精度相对较高；比较大的弓弩，射程可以达到900米，这样的射程甚至优于今天的某些手枪。

秦军大型弓的弓干长176.1厘米，直径4.5厘米，弦长140厘米，杀伤力很强。出土的数以万计的铜镞，除有一支较为特别的双翼镞外，其余都是三棱镞和在此基础上增强的三出刃镞。秦军大量装备了当时最

exclusive crossbowman army found in Pit No.2. Without sabres, the Qin cavalrymen "hold reins on one hand while the other hand remains the pose of bow-grasping", indicating that the major weapons are bows and arrows. Based on that, it is clear that bow, crossbow and arrow play major and indispensable roles for Qin's troop.

The crossbows from the mausoleum are classified into two major types according to the size. The small one is mainly applied for shoot within short distance whose range is 150 metres, with relatively high accuracy; the large one can cover a range of 900 metres and the performance of some modern pistols can not be compared with that of the crossbow.

The large bow of the Qin Dynasty is a very destructive weapon, consisted of the 176.1 centimetres long curved elastic limbs, a 140 centimetres long bowstring and the length between the handle and bowstring is 4.5 centimetres. Among the tens of thousands of bronze arrowheads, except for one with special leaf-shaped arrowhead, the rest are all with three-ridge arrowhead and enhanced three-blade arrowhead. Qin's troop was equipped with plentiful and the most advanced arrowheads at that time, which ensured the arrows to fly stably and largely raised the shooting precision. In

• **秦陵中出土的铜戈**

戈是中国所特有的长兵器，具有横击、钩援等多种格斗功能。在中国古代，干与戈合称"干戈"，是各种兵器的统称。成语"大动干戈"指的就是动用武器，发动战争。

Bronze Dagger-axe Unearthed from the Mausoleum of Qin Shihuang

As a long weapon peculiar to China, the dagger-axe obtains many assault functions including hooking and hitting. In ancient China, the *Gan* (an ancient weapon) and the *Ge* (dagger-axe) usually came together, called *Gange*, representing all weapons. The idiom "take up *Gange*" refers to employ weapons to wage a war.

- **秦陵中出土的铜矛**

  矛是一种用于直刺和扎挑的长柄兵器，是古代军队中使用时间最长的冷兵器之一。

  Bronze Spears Unearthed from the Mausoleum of Qin Shihuang

  Spears are weapons with long handle used to thrust and stick the enemy, known as one of the cold weapons with the longest history.

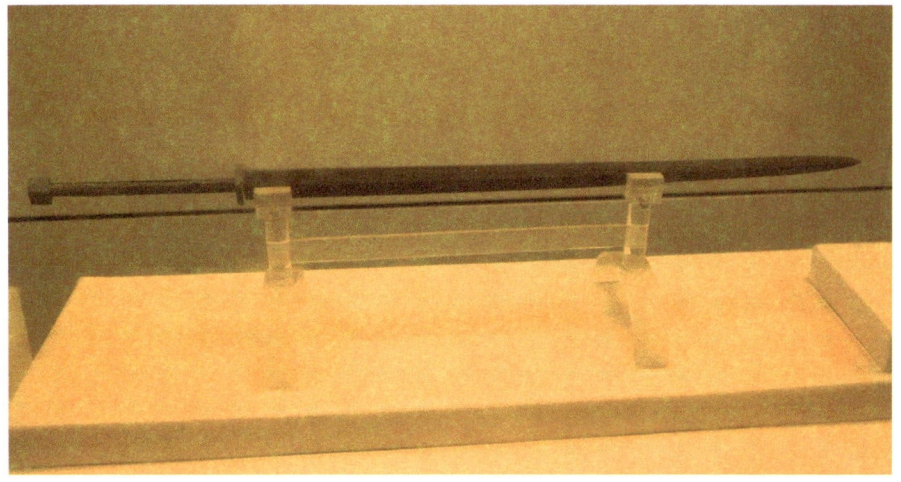

- **秦陵中出土的铜剑**

  剑是古代常用的短兵器之一，剑直身，尖峰，两侧有刃，后安短柄，常配有剑鞘，素有"百兵之君"的美称。

  Bronze Sword Unearthed from the Mausoleum of Qin Shihuang

  The sword is a frequently-used ancient short weapon. It has straight body and sharp double edged blade. The blade is connected with a short hilt and normally a scabbard is equipped with a sword. The sword enjoys the title of the Emperor of Weapons.

流行的箭镞，箭镞飞行稳定，射击精度有了大大地改善。在考古发掘中，考古学家们还发现了一种特大的镞，长达41厘米，重约100克，是用大型的强弩发射的。这种镞的杀伤力非常惊人，具有很强的威慑力。

秦陵中出土的长兵器主要有

addition, archaeologists found a type of extra-large arrowheads of 41 centimetres long and approximately 100 grams weight, used especially for large crossbows. This ancient mass destructive weapon would undoubtedly pose horrible threats and deterrent force to the enemy.

The long weapons in the Mausoleum of Qin Shihuang are mainly spears, *Ji* (halberds), long swords and *Pi* (long lance), all made out of bronze. The spears excavated from the tomb are normally 7 metres long. Soldiers who used spears combated cooperatively in order to increase the lethality. *Ji* has a normal length of 3.5 metres and this weapon allows the soldier to fight individually. The metal part of *Pi's* head is similar to sword whose length is about 30 centimetres, linked with a

矛、戟、长剑和铍等，这些兵器的制作材料均为青铜。秦陵中出土的矛通身长7米左右，手持这种矛的士兵一般是依靠协同作战的方阵来获得冲击力。戟一般通身长3.5米，使用这种长度兵器的战士一般注重于单兵格斗。铍的头部金属部分和剑相似，长约30厘米，装有长约3米的柄，是一种锐利的刺杀兵器。

秦陵出土的这些青铜兵器，制作非常考究，做工十分精良，尤其是剑、矛、镞等，在地下埋藏两千多年，有些仍然完好如新。据考证，秦人的冶炼技术和兵器锻造水平已经达到了较高的水平。秦俑坑中出土的青铜兵器所呈现出来的防锈技术已非常高超，秦人在一些青铜兵器中广泛采用了"含铬化合物氧化层"的防锈处理方法，来长久保持兵器不被腐蚀。秦军的青铜兵器经光谱和化学分析，主要成分是铜锡合金，并含有微量的镍、镁、铝、锌、硅、锰、铊、钼、钒、钴、铬、铌等元素。秦人在锻造兵器的时候，根据兵器的不同用途，相应地变化兵器的金属配方，以增强兵器的杀伤力。如秦军的青铜镞

3-metre-long handle, served as a sharp thrusting weapon.

The unearthed bronze weapons from the Mausoleum of Qin Shihuang are quite exquisite in manufacture whose details are meticulously presented. Especially for swords, spears and arrowheads, it is amazing that after more than 2,000 years, some of them are still intact as new. According to research, the metal melting technique and weapon forging technique in the Qin Dynasty (221 B.C.-206 B.C.) had reached a relatively high level. The unearthed bronze weapons from the tomb demonstrate the extremely advanced rust-proof technique. The "oxide layer containing chromium compound" which were widely spread and adopted can provide protection for the ancient weapons from rusting away for a long period of time. According to spectral and chemical analyses, the main composition of bronze weapons in the Qin Dynasty is copper and tin alloy, mixed with tiny amounts of nickel, magnesium, aluminium, zinc, silicon, manganese, thallium, molybdenum, vanadium, cobalt, chromium and niobium. Differing in usage, the Qin's craftsmen would change and adjust the proportions of different metals in order to enhance and increase the lethality. For instance,

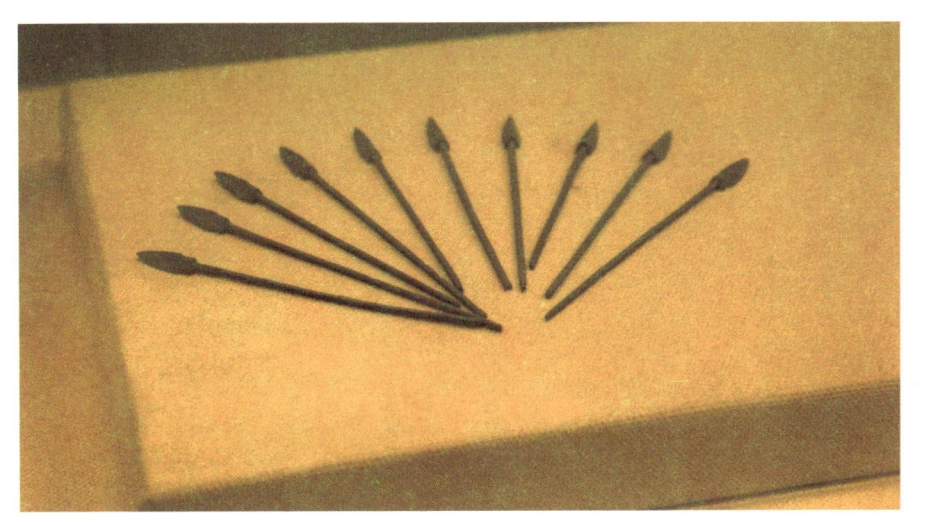

• 秦陵中出土的铜箭镞
Bronze Arrowheads Unearthed from the Mausoleum of Qin Shihuang

中铅含量的比例较大。众所周知，铅金属有较大的毒性，一旦含铅的箭头射入人体，可使人体中毒，加速人的死亡。

the proportion of lead within the bronze arrowheads of Qin's troop is comparatively high since lead is toxic and once shot people, this arrowhead could poison them and accelerate the death speed.

> 铜水禽

　　铜禽坑位于秦陵东北角，与秦始皇陵中心相距约1500米，是目前所发现距秦陵最远的一个陪葬坑。2001年，秦陵铜禽坑出土了14只青铜水禽。2002年，又有31只青铜水禽相继出土。秦陵中出土的青铜水禽主要分为三种，即仙鹤、天鹅和大雁。出土的青铜水禽姿态各异，或两两相对、曲颈扬首，或脚踩祥云、直立回望，或低头饮水、啄虫嬉戏……

　　在中国传统文化中，仙鹤象征着幸福、吉祥、长寿和忠贞。仙鹤在中国的文学和美术作品中屡有出现，殷商时代的墓葬中就有鹤的雕塑。春秋战国时期的青铜器中，鹤形礼器也已出现。秦始皇在自己统治生涯的末期，迷信长寿和成仙。

> Bronze Waterfowl

Located in the northeast, the pit of bronze waterfowl is 1.5 kilometres away from the central of Mausoleum of Qin Shihuang, known as the most remote pit of the imperial tomb. In 2001, 14 bronze waterfowls were excavated from this pit and in 2002, another 31 were found. The major 3 types of these unearthed bronze waterfowls are cranes, swans and wild geese. The bronze waterfowls are presented in different poses: some are face to face in a pair; some curve their necks and raise their heads; some step on auspicious clouds; some bow their heads and drink water; some catch worms for fun; etc.

　　In traditional Chinese culture, the crane is the symbol of happiness, auspiciousness, longevity and loyalty. It is quite common to see the emergence of crane in Chinese literature and paintings and early in the Shang Dynasty, the statues of crane were

而在中国古代的传说中，仙鹤又都是作为仙人的坐骑而出现的。因而执着于长寿和成仙的秦始皇选择了仙鹤作为陪葬，大概是想借鹤为舆，腾云升天。

中国古代称天鹅为"鹄"，被认为是天的使者，是一种神鸟。秦始皇在自己的陵墓中设置了天鹅，似乎是在营造一种神秘的"天境"，借以显示自己身份的尊贵。

中国古人认为大雁有仁者之心。一个雁群中，年老病弱的大雁飞行较慢，其余强壮的同伴不会弃之不顾。同时，大雁一雌一雄两两相配，从一而终，这是有情有义的表现。迁徙中的雁阵飞行时排成队列，整齐有序，其中青壮年的大雁不会超越到带头的老雁之前，这是恭谦有礼的象征。无论是飞行还是落地歇息，雁群中都会有十分敏锐机警的壮雁负责警戒，这体现了大雁的智慧。因此，大雁成为最受中国人喜爱和尊敬的禽鸟之一。

青铜水禽的出土反映了秦人"事死如事生"的思想观念。同时有考古队专家认为，如此众多青

included in the funeral objects. In the Spring and Autumn Period and Warring States Period, the crane shaped sacrificial vessels had appeared. During the last phase of Qin Shihuang's domination, he pursued longevity and hoped to become immortal. According to ancient Chinese legend, the celestial beings normally appear riding on cranes. Therefore, Qin Shihuang chose the image of crane as the model of his funeral objects and hoped to depend on the power of this creature to realise his dream of longevity and immortalization.

In ancient China, the swan was called *Hu*. Ancient Chinese people regarded the swan as the messenger from heaven, worshiped it as an immortal bird. The statues of swan found in the mausoleum of Qin Shihuang indicate that it seems the Emperor tried to create a mystical fairyland to manifest his dignity.

People in ancient time believed that the wild goose is the representative of mercy since the old and weak wild geese within a flock will not be discarded by the strong ones. At the same time, the wild geese exist in pairs of one female and one male and they are faithful to each other forever, which is also a proof of their sentiment and loyalty. During the migration, the wild geese fly in neat and orderly array and the

铜水禽的出土，尤其是青铜天鹅的出土，使人们得知这个陪葬坑营造出了某种"水环境"。这种"水环境"的发现，让秦陵的墓葬形态更为完整。

strong and young ones would never fly in advance of the leading old ones, showing their courtesy and politeness. No matter it is during flying or landing for a rest, the strong wild geese will perform as observant and vigilant guards for the flock, which presents this creature's wisdom. Therefore, the wild geese are one of the birds that are the most favored and respected by Chinese people.

The excavated bronze waterfowls reflect the ideology "honoring the dead as the living" of people in the Qin Dynasty. The archaeologists also consider that among the large numbers of bronze waterfowls, especially for the unearthed bronze swans, this pit of the mausoleum constructs a certain atmosphere known as the "water environment". The emergence of "water environment" integrates the whole Mausoleum of Qin Shihuang.

- 青铜鹤
  Bronze Crane